DIABETIC BAKING COOKBOOK

100 Homemade Sugar Free Recipes from Sweet and Savory Bread to Pies

TABLE OF CONTENTS

INTRODUCTION

The concept of a Diabetic diet has been of interest to a large number of people who have chosen the path of a healthy diet and lifestyle for many centuries. This is because, no matter how tasty many of our dishes are, many of the foods we eat are unhealthy. They contain few nutrients, they are in excess of carbohydrates and, of course, this slowly disrupts the functioning of the internal organs and delicate systems of the body. Various diseases, such as obesity, diabetes mellitus, diseases of the cardiovascular and digestive systems, as well as cancer and endocrine disruption, were scientifically associated with a change in our genes or a violation of the physiology of the body as a result of the foods we consume.

Of the popular foods, the Diabetic diet rules do not allow you to eat foods such as pastries made from wheat flour and other high-carb ingredients, legumes, grains, starchy vegetables, such as carrots, beets. and corn, any form of sugar, high-carb fruits, potatoes, root vegetables, and alcohol. Most nutritionists recommend a low-carb diet. Diabetic diet is able to solve the issue in a healthy way according to the plan of consumed products, variety of dishes, and without loss of taste.

You may not be accustomed to getting used to baking from the allowed list of ingredients, but believe me, such bread and sweets allow you to eat a piece of bread at breakfast and with your favorite soup.

Refusing warm and soft bread and pastries can be difficult for most people. With this cookbook, you no longer have to say goodbye to delicious pastries.

In this Diabetic Bakery cookbook, you'll learn how to make low-carb pastries that will seduce your taste buds.

CHAPTER 1 GUIDE TO BASIC INGREDIENTS AND TIPS FOR DIABETIC BAKING

Enjoy delicious bread; it's not just eating store bread with sausage to quickly satisfy your hunger. To enjoy homemade cakes is to see the consistency and to feel the aroma while taking care of the health of your family. You can make bread in the form of a cake or a loaf, experiment with recipes, add spices, nuts, or fruits. The process of making homemade bread is very exciting, and you do not need to have the experience of a chef in baking.

You do not need to give up your favorite bread and delicious pastries with an alluring aroma if you are on a diet. Just use unique ingredients that match the diabetic diet.

Basic Ingredients for Diabetic Baking

Coconut Flour

Coconut flour contains about 75% fiber in composition. This is about 9–10 grams for every two tablespoons, which diminishes the absorption of sugar into the circulatory system. It is gotten from pounding the dried white interior meat of the coconut. It is additionally quite tricky to work with and requires consistent practice to get a perfect bread using it, due to its ability to absorb eggs and oil — essentially, anything that is wet—more like an insatiable sponge, absorbing fluids until it is a soaked clump of porridge.

Hence, it can't be effectively tweaked without altering the fluid ratio of the recipe. This may have a domino impact on the quality and effectiveness of other ingredients in the recipe.

It is ideal to follow the recipe precisely until you are comfortable enough to try different things by tweaking the recipes. Coconut flour is certifiably not a critical source of protein in bread recipes but contains lauric acid with antiviral and antifungal properties. Its fragrant, smooth, somewhat sweet nature adds a special component even though small quantities are utilized. It additionally has the awesome nature of fulfilling our hunger cravings for a longer time. Coconut flour is incredibly high in fiber and low in edible carbs. Because it's so high in fiber, it is perfect to be used in preparing weight loss meals. Research has really shown that eating a meal with a quarter cup of coconut flour can diminish caloric stores by as much as 10 percent.

Almond Flour

Almond flour is purely finely ground whole blanched almonds (without the skin), enriched with essential vitamins and minerals, and high in protein and fiber. Almond meal can be likened to the consistency of cornmeal. Most almond flour brands are more coarsely ground, which influences the final texture in baked products. In thick or brisk-type bread, this doesn't generally make a difference. However, when we're trying to achieve more tender loaf— white bread, Challah, French-style—the appearance and taste response are important.

Search for brands that show they are finely ground. They are pricier, but you will be more joyful with the finished product.

Natural Whey Protein Powder

This obviously cannot be described as flour for any reason; however, to make diabetic bread, it is an incredible substitution. Whey is the fluid that is left after the main phases of cheese production and then processed into a concentrated powder. It is viewed as total protein and contains every one of the nine essential amino acids. Studies have proven that, in addition to improving muscle quality (which helps the muscle to burn more calories), these essential amino acids help avert cardiovascular diseases, diabetes, and age-related bone loss. And there's more—from anti-cancer properties to improving food reaction in kids with asthma. Even though It must be enhanced with our other flours, it breaks down rapidly to help make delectable, healthy, nutrient-rich baked products.

Golden Flaxseed Meal

Golden flaxseed originates from a delicate wildflower with beautiful, pure, light blue blooms. The fruit is a little pod that contains modest, polished seeds loaded with omega–3 fatty acids, fiber, antioxidants, essential vitamins, and minerals. It is the only flour known to possess zero net carbs (That is, after subtracting the grams of fiber from a similar number of carbohydrates) and has a lot of therapeutic benefits.

One exciting discovery I made was that the texture of the bread is significantly improved if the Golden flaxseed meal is further refined in the blender.

At times I come across concerns with respect to four potential health issues if a lot of flaxseed meal is consumed. Various studies, in any case, report practically no issues from eating it but rather lists its numerous advantages. Three cyanogenic glycosides contained in flaxseed—additionally present in broccoli, kale, and cabbage, among others— cease to exist when it is baked. Another study revealed that an individual would need to consume in excess of 8 cups per day to cause toxicity. A large portion of the recipes that include ground flaxseed utilizes just ½ cup for the whole loaf, which can be calculated to be around two tablespoons of flaxseed in two servings.

I accept that too much of any good thing can cause problems. I would likewise not prescribe eating flax seeds wholly, from a nutritional and digestive standpoint.

If you would, in any case, rather substitute one of the different flours, you may have the best accomplishment with almond dinner, finely ground. Ground flaxseed is a magnificent wellspring of fundamental supplements and adds a tasty nutty flavor to baked merchandise. Nutritionally both the brilliant and dull assortments are the equivalent.

Egg Whites

Having lots of egg whites in a recipe are genuinely economical and simple to plan. I get them in two different ways; in powder form in a 36-ounce canister that equals 255 egg whites and; in the fluid form, which can be bought with discounts at stores like Costco or 1-quart containers in nearby staple goods. I have seen wide varieties in cost, so be sure to compare before buying. Since they are pasteurized, they won't whip so well as new whites, however adding a small quantity of cream of tartar will make excellent, fluffy steeps similarly as high as using fresh egg whites.

Egg whites are essentially 90% water and 10% proteins, which are long chains of amino acids. When we beat air into the whites, these chains become denatured, which implies they unwind and stretch into shapes that trap air, making light textures in what we bake. There is a school of thought that heating/cooking protein—which includes protein powders like whey—decimates the nutritional worth because our bodies can't assimilate "denatured" foods. This is false. If that were the case, we would need to eat everything raw, right?! Eggs, meat, all that we cook and prepare are denatured when warmed. The food leaves the stove changed in appearance, yet the protein isn't denatured; rather than being folded into tight molecular balls, the protein chains become long strands.

Oat Fiber

Oat fiber is a powdered fiber. It is pure fiber, not a flour. It is used as filler because carbohydrate and calorie content is zero per ounce.

Chocolate and Coconut Products

Ideally, you should use dark chocolate bars when baking. Dark chocolate has 86% cocoa powder. Go for dark types and unsweetened ones to control the sweetness. Cocoa powder is excellent for baked or non-baked goods like cookies, puddings, and cakes. Coconut oil can be used in place of standard oils used in baked bread and other baked products. Coconut oil reduces your hunger and can keep you fuller for longer.

Fruits

You can use low carb fruits in sugar-free baking. Some low-carb fruit options include grapefruit, watermelon, casaba melon, starfruit, rhubarb, peaches, and berries.

Nuts

Nuts and seeds are accepted in the Diabetic diet. They also offer you with many health benefits. Almonds are delicious, crunchy, and gives you texture to almost any bread. You can also make nut butter with almonds. Macadamia nuts are high in fat, and you can bake them in brownies or sprinkle them in cream cheese. The walnuts are also another choice. They are soft and more decadent and great for sprinkling. Pecans are another good choice. If you are baking muffins, cupcakes, pancakes, waffles, or even bread, you can use pecans.

Chia seeds are high in fat and low on carbs. They are also packed with phosphorus, calcium, and magnesium.

Pumpkin Seed/Sunflower Seed Meal

These low carb flours are rich in vitamins and minerals like Vitamin E, copper, thiamine, selenium, and phosphorus. These flours can conveniently replace almond meal or almond flour in any recipe. You can use a food processor or coffee grinder to make your own homemade pumpkin seed or sunflower meals. Pumpkin and sunflower seeds meal can be stored in a cool, dark pantry for up to 4 months.

Psyllium Husk (Whole and Ground, Unflavored)

Unflavored psyllium hunks are sold both whole and as a ground powder. Powdered psyllium makes for dense bread. Psyllium seed husk helps to produce a bread-like texture, as it replaces gluten to a certain extent. The husk is highly absorbent, so although the bread will not have the same airy texture as gluten-rich bread, its inclusion produces a moisture loaf. There is no carbohydrate content since the husk is pure fiber.

Low Carb Sweeteners

Erythritol

Erythritol, a sugar alcohol produced naturally in fruits and from fermentation, is an exceptional natural and healthy low-carb sweetener that has bulking properties, which make it perfect for baking. Erythritol is a sweetener that leaves no aftertaste, and it is also easy on the stomach. Erythritol and erythritol blends can be used in diabetic snacks and desserts. Natvia, a blend of erythritol and stevia, is also liberally used in many recipes. One of the many features of erythritol is that is doesn't attract moisture.

Stevia

Stevia is a natural and healthy low carb sweetener derived from plants. Stevia has zero impact on blood sugar. Stevia is a great source of magnesium, zinc, potassium, vitamin B3, and 150 times sweetener than matching amounts of sugar. However, stevia has a strong aftertaste and can only be used in very small amounts is certain recipes or as a blend with erythritol.

Xylitol

Xylitol is another often used natural sweetener with no after taste. Xylitol contains anti-bacterial properties that protect the mouth from bacteria that cause tooth decay. Xylitol is also used to manage mid-ear infections. However, use Xylitol is small quantities to avoid gastrointestinal discomfort. Keep this product away from dogs because it is toxic to dogs.

Swerve

Swerve or a blend of oligosaccharides and erythritol is a natural and healthy low carb sweetener that has zero impact on blood sugar. Swerve can be added into tea or coffee with no aftertaste and can also be used to cook. Swerve can be used to replace sugar in any recipe, as the same amounts of sugar and swerve have equal sweetness.

Natvia

Natvia, a blend of stevia and erythritol, is also a natural sweetener. Natvia eliminates the intense aftertaste of stevia, yet retaining its sweetness and combining it with the bulking properties of erythritol to make a perfect healthy low carb sweetener suitable for baking.

Benefits of Home-Baked Bread

1. Lower cost: Baking your own bread can help lower the cost.

2. Better taste: You bake your own bread. So you can adjust bread ingredients and make the bread tastier.

3. More nutrition: Store brought bread is unimpressive when it comes to nutrition. Store brought bread offers more filler ingredients and less nutrition. On the other hand, home baked bread offers more nutrition.

4. Custom recipes: You can adjust ingredients and create bread from custom recipes.

5. Enjoyment: You can enjoy the whole process of baking warm, flavorful, and delicious bread in your home.

6. Homemade bread is guaranteed fresh: You are making your own bread, so it is always fresh.

7. No more harmful preservatives: Often store brought bread has harmful ingredients. By baking at home, you can avoid these preservatives.

Useful Tips for Diabetic Baking

1. Always sift your flour before start making your bread.
2. Avoid glass pans because they are poor conductors of heat. This causes your bread to be cooked before time.
3. If you don't have baking powder, you can use the combination of baking soda, lemon juice, and citric acid. Use 2 Tbsp. lemon juice with a single tsp. of baking soda.
4. Choose ingredients which are more natural and close to the source.
5. Add a pinch salt to counter the aftertaste of some sweeteners such as stevia. Some mix stevia and erythritol for better result.
6. The oven temperature and time to heat up may vary depending on oven model. Some models are more efficient than others. So don't solely depend on the recipe's stated cooking time.
7. Use butter or coconut oil to grease your baking pan. Also, double-grease by creating two layers on it.
8. Let your bread cool before slicing. The bread will get firmer when it is cooler.

Here are Some More Tips

- Read the instructions: Read the recipe instructions and follow them carefully.
- Lay it all out: Gather all the ingredients on your work station before starting baking bread.
- Buy a digital scale: A few ounces or few grams can make a big difference. You need to measure everything precisely. So buy a digital scale.
- Keep your eye on the oven: Don't leave your bread in the oven and forgot about it.
- Write in your bread diary: Write your experiences in your bread diary.
- Master a basic recipe, then experiment: You need to master basic bread recipes then move onto more complex ones.

CHAPTER 2 BREAD RECIPES

Sandwich Bread

Prep time: 5 minutes
Cook time: 1 hour
Servings: 12

Ingredients

- 1 tsp. apple cider vinegar
- ¾ cup water
- ¼ cup avocado oil
- 5 eggs
- ½ tsp. salt
- 1 tsp. baking soda
- ½ cup coconut flour
- 2 cups plus 2 tbsp. almond flour

Method

1. Preheat the oven to 350F. Grease a loaf pan.
2. In a bowl, whisk almond flour, coconut flour, and salt.
3. In another bowl, separate the egg whites from egg yolks. Set egg whites aside.
4. In a blender, blend the oil, egg yolks, water, vinegar, and baking soda for 5 minutes on medium speed until combined.
5. Let the mixture sit for 1 minute then add in the reserved egg whites and mix until frothy, about 10 to 15 seconds.
6. Add the dry ingredients and process on high for 5 to 10 seconds before batter becomes too thick for the blender. Blend until the batter is smooth.
7. Transfer batter into the greased loaf pan and smoothen the top.
8. Bake in the oven until a skewer inserted comes out clean, about 50 to 70 minutes.
9. Cool, slice, and serve.

Nutritional Facts Per Serving

- Calories: 200g
- Fat: 7g
- Carb: 7g
- Protein: 16g

Chia Seed Bread

Prep time: 10 minutes
Cook time: 40 minutes
Servings: 16 slices

Ingredients

- ½ tsp. xanthan gum
- ½ cup butter
- 2 tbsp. coconut oil
- 1 tbsp. baking powder
- 3 tbsp. sesame seeds
- 2 tbsp. chia seeds
- ½ tsp. salt
- ¼ cup sunflower seeds
- 2 cups almond flour
- 7 eggs

Method

1. Preheat the oven to 350F.
2. Beat eggs in a bowl on high for 1 to 2 minutes.
3. Beat in the xanthan gum and combine coconut oil and melted butter into eggs, beating continuously.
4. Set aside the sesame seeds, but add the rest of the ingredients.
5. Line a loaf pan with baking paper. Place the mixture in it. Top the mixture with sesame seeds.
6. Bake in the oven until a toothpick inserted comes out clean, about 35 to 40 minutes.

Nutritional Facts Per Serving

- Calories: 405
- Fat: 37g
- Carb: 4g
- Protein: 14g

Flax Bread

Prep time: 10 minutes
Cook time: 18 to 20 minutes
Servings: 8

Ingredients

- ¾ cup of water
- 1 ½ cups ground flax seeds
- ½ cup psyllium husk powder
- 1 tbsp. baking powder
- 7 large egg whites
- 3 tbsp. butter
- 2 tsp. salt
- ¼ cup granulated stevia
- 1 large whole egg
- 1 ½ cups whey protein isolate

Method

1. Preheat the oven to 350F.
2. Combine together whey protein isolate, psyllium husk, baking powder, sweetener, and salt.
3. In another bowl, mix together the water, butter, egg, and egg whites.
4. Slowly add psyllium husk mixture to egg mixture and mix well.
5. Lightly grease a bread pan with butter and pour in the batter.
6. Bake in the oven until the bread is set, about 18 to 20 minutes.

Nutritional Facts Per Serving

- Calories: 265.5
- Fat: 15.68g
- Carb: 1.88g
- Protein:24.34 g

Coconut Flour Almond Bread

Prep time: 10 minutes
Cook time: 30 minutes
Servings: 4

Ingredients

- 1 tbsp. butter, melted
- 1 tbsp. coconut oil, melted
- 6 eggs
- 1 tsp. baking soda
- 2 tbsp. ground flaxseed
- 1 ½ tbsp. psyllium husk powder
- 5 tbsp. coconut flour
- 1 ½ cup almond flour

Method

1. Preheat the oven to 400F.
2. Mix the eggs in a bowl for a few minutes.
3. Add in the butter and coconut oil and mix once more for 1 minute.
4. Add the almond flour, coconut flour, baking soda, psyllium husk, and ground flaxseed to the mixture. Let sit for 15 minutes.
5. Lightly grease the loaf pan with coconut oil. Pour the mixture in the pan.
6. Place in the oven and bake until a toothpick inserted in it comes out dry, about 25 minutes.

Nutritional Facts Per Serving

- Calories: 475
- Fat: 38g
- Carb: 7g
- Protein: 19g

Bakers Bread

Prep time: 10 minutes
Cook time: 20 minutes
Servings: 12

Ingredients

- Pinch of salt
- 4 tbsp. light cream cheese, softened
- ½ tsp. cream of tartar
- 4 eggs, yolks, and whites separated

Method

1. Heat 2 racks in the middle of the oven at 350F.
2. Line 2 baking pan with parchment paper, then grease with cooking spray.
3. Separate egg yolks from the whites. Place in separate mixing bowls.
4. Beat the egg whites and cream of tartar with a hand mixer until stiff, about 3 to 5 minutes. Do not over-beat.
5. Whisk the cream cheese, salt, and egg yolks until smooth.
6. Slowly fold the cheese mix into the whites until fluffy.
7. Spoon ¼ cup measure of the batter onto the baking sheets, 6 mounds on each sheet.
8. Bake in the oven for 20 to 22 minutes, alternating racks halfway through.
9. Cool and serve.

Nutritional Facts Per Serving

- Calories: 41
- Fat: 3.2g
- Carb: 1g
- Protein: 2.4g

Blueberry Bread Loaf

Prep time: 20 minutes
Cook time: 65 minutes
Servings: 12

Ingredients for the bread dough

- 10 tbsp. coconut flour
- 9 tbsp. melted butter
- 2/3 cup granulates swerve sweetener
- 1 ½ tsp. baking powder
- 2 tbsp. heavy whipping cream
- 1 ½ tsp. vanilla extract
- ½ tsp. cinnamon
- 2 tbsp. sour cream
- 6 large eggs
- ½ tsp. salt
- ¾ cup blueberries

For the topping

- 1 tbsp. heavy whipping cream
- 2 tbsp. confectioner swerve sweetener
- 1 tsp. melted butter
- 1/8 tsp. vanilla extract
- ¼ tsp. lemon zest

Method

1. Preheat the oven to 350F. Line a loaf pan with baking paper.
2. In a bowl, mix granulated swerve, heavy whipping cream, eggs, and baking powder.
3. Once combined, add the butter, vanilla extract, salt, cinnamon, and sour cream. Then add the coconut flour to the batter.
4. Pour a layer about ½ inch of dough into the bread pan. Place ¼ cup blueberries on top of the dough. Keep repeating until the dough and blueberry layers are complete.
5. Bake for 65 to 75 minutes.
6. Meanwhile, in a bowl, beat the vanilla extract, butter, heavy whipping cream, lemon zest, and confectioner swerve. Mix until creamy.
7. Cool the bread once baked. Then drizzle the icing topping on the bread.
8. Slice and serve.

Nutritional Facts Per Serving

- Calories: 155
- Fat: 13g
- Carb: 4g
- Protein: 3g

Cloud Bread Cheese

Prep time: 5 minutes
Cook time: 30 minutes
Servings: 12

Ingredients for cream cheese filling

- 1 egg yolk
- ½ tsp. vanilla stevia drops for filling
- 8 oz. softened cream cheese

Base egg dough

- ½ tsp. cream of tartar
- 1 tbsp. coconut flour
- ¼ cup unflavored whey protein
- 3 oz. softened cream cheese
- ¼ tsp. vanilla stevia drops for dough
- 4 eggs, separated

Method

1. Preheat the oven to 325F.
2. Line two baking sheets with parchment paper.
3. In a bowl, stir the 8 ounces cream cheese, stevia, and egg yolk.
4. Transfer to the pastry bag.
5. In another bowl, separate egg yolks from whites.
6. Add 3 oz. cream cheese, yolks, stevia, whey protein, and coconut flour. Mix until smooth.
7. Whip cream of tartar with the egg whites until stiff peaks form.
8. Fold in the yolk/cream cheese mixture into the beaten whites.
9. Spoon batter onto each baking sheet, 6 mounds on each. Press each mound to flatten a bit.
10. Add cream cheese filling in the middle of each batter.
11. Bake for 30 minutes at 325F.

Nutritional Facts Per Serving

- Calories: 120
- Fat: 10.7g
- Carb: 1.1g
- Protein: 5.4g

Cauliflower Bread Loaf

Prep time: 1 hour 10 minutes
Cook time: 45 minutes
Servings: 10

Ingredients for the bread dough

- 1 ¼ cups of almond flour
- 3 cup of riced cauliflower
- 1 tbsp. baking powder
- 6 tbsp. of olive oil
- 6 large eggs, separated
- 1 tsp. salt

Optional flavorings

- dried or fresh herbs
- shredded parmesan or cheddar cheese
- garlic powder or minced garlic

Method

1. Preheat the oven to 350F. Line a bread loaf with baking paper.
2. Place cauliflower into the small pot to steam until it becomes tender. Place it to the side.
3. Cream the whites of the eggs in a food processor for 4 minutes. Set to the side.
4. In a bowl, whisk the egg yolks, and almond flour until mixed well. Next, add the baking powder, oil, and salt and mix until smooth.
5. Remove excess fluid from the cooled cauliflower with a paper towel.
6. Stir in the dried cauliflower and mix well. Add the flavoring ingredients.
7. In small amounts, fold the egg white mixture to the mixture until fluffy. Don't overbeat.
8. Transfer the dough into the bread loaf pan.
9. Bake in the oven for 45 minutes. Test with a knife.
10. Cool, slice, and serve.

Nutritional Facts Per Serving

- Calories: 155
- Fat: 13g
- Carb: 4g
- Protein: 3g

Cheese and Bacon Bread Loaf

Prep time: 1 hour
Cook time: 45 to 50 minutes
Servings: 10

Ingredients

- 1/3 cup sour cream
- 4 tbsp. melted butter
- 1 ½ cups almond flour
- 1 cup grated cheese
- 1 tbsp. baking powder
- 2 large eggs
- 7 ounces bacon

Method

1. Preheat oven to 300F. Line the loaf pan with baking paper.
2. Cut and dice the bacon and cook until crispy.
3. In a bowl, mix almond flour and baking powder with a fork.
4. Using a hand mixer, cream the sour cream and eggs into the flour mix. Add to the mixed dry ingredients along with cooled butter and combine well.
5. Fold in the grated cheese and cooked bacon into the dough.
6. Empty the dough into the bread loaf pan. Sprinkle the top with extra cheese if you want the bread to be extra cheesy.
7. Bake in the oven for 45 to 50 minutes.
8. Cool, slice, and serve.

Nutritional Facts Per Serving

- Calories: 292
- Fat: 13g
- Carb: 4g
- Protein: 3g

Savory Bread Loaf

Prep time: 1 minutes
Cook time: 50 to 55 minutes
Servings: 12

Ingredients

- ¼ cup coconut flour
- 8 eggs
- 8 ounces cream cheese
- 2 ½ cups almond flour
- ½ cup butter
- 1 tsp. rosemary
- 1 ½ tsp. baking powder
- 1 tsp. sage
- 2 tbsp. parsley

Method

1. Preheat the oven to 350F. Line a loaf pan with parchment paper.
2. In a bowl, combine the butter, rosemary, parsley, sage, and sour cream until fluffy and mixed well.
3. In the mixture, whisk each egg and repeat until all eggs are mixed into the mixture and are smooth.
4. Add the almond and coconut flour and the baking powder and combine them thoroughly resulting in a thick dough.
5. Pour the completed dough in the lined bread loaf pan.
6. Heat the bread loaf in the stove for 50 to 55 minutes. Check the middle to ensure it is baked properly.

Nutritional Facts Per Serving

- Calories: 202
- Fat: 20g
- Carb: 5g
- Protein: 6g

Quick Low-Carb Bread Loaf

Prep time: 45 minutes
Cook time: 40 to 45 minutes
Servings: 16

Ingredients

- 2/3 cup coconut flour
- ½ cup butter, melted
- 3 tbsp. coconut oil, melted
- 1 1/3 cup almond flour
- ½ tsp. xanthan gum
- 1 tsp. baking powder
- 6 large eggs
- ½ tsp. salt

Method

1. Preheat the oven to 350F. Cover the bread loaf pan with baking paper.
2. Beat the eggs until creamy.
3. Add in the coconut flour and almond flour, mixing them for 1 minute. Next, add the xanthan gum, coconut oil, baking powder, butter, and salt and mix them until the dough turns thick.
4. Put the completed dough into the prepared line of the bread loaf pan.
5. Place in oven. Bake for 40 to 45 minutes. Check with a knife.
6. Slice and serve.

Nutritional Facts Per Serving

- Calories: 174
- Fat: 15g
- Carb: 5g
- Protein: 5g

Low Carb Bread

Prep time: 10 minutes
Cook time: 21 minutes
Servings: 12

Ingredients

- 2 cups mozzarella cheese, grated
- 8 oz. cream cheese
- Herbs and spices to taste
- 1 tbsp. baking powder
- 1 cup crushed pork rinds
- ¼ cup parmesan cheese, grated
- 3 large eggs

Method

1. Preheat oven to 375F.
2. Line parchment paper over the baking pan.
3. In a bowl, place cream cheese and mozzarella and microwave for 1 minute on high power. Stir and microwave for 1 minute more. Then stir again.
4. Stir in egg, parmesan, pork rinds, herbs, spices and baking powder until mixed.
5. Spread mixture on the baking pan and bake until top is lightly brown, about 15 to 20 minutes.
6. Cool, slice, and serve.

Nutritional Facts Per Serving

- Calories: 166
- Fat: 13g
- Carb: 1g
- Protein: 9g

Fluffy Paleo Bread

Prep time: 10 minutes
Cook time: 40 minutes
Servings: 15

Ingredients

- 1 ¼ cup almond flour
- 5 eggs
- 1 tsp. lemon juice
- 1/3 cup avocado oil
- 1 dash black pepper
- ½ tsp. sea salt
- 3 to 4 tbsp. tapioca flour
- 1 to 2 tsp. poppy seed
- ¼ cup ground flaxseed
- ½ tsp. baking soda

Top with

- Poppy seeds
- Pumpkin seeds

Method

1. Preheat the oven to 350F.
2. Line a baking pan with parchment paper. Set aside.
3. In a bowl, add eggs, avocado oil, and lemon juice and whisk until combined.
4. In another bowl, add tapioca flour, almond flour, baking soda, flaxseed, black pepper and poppy seed. Mix.
5. Add the lemon juice mixture into the flour mixture and mix well.
6. Add the batter into the prepared loaf pan and top with extra pumpkin seeds and poppy seeds.
7. Cover loaf pan and transfer into the prepared oven.
8. Bake for 20 minutes. Remove cover and bake until an inserted knife comes out clean, after about 15 to 20 minutes.
9. Remove from oven and cool.
10. Slice and serve.

Nutritional Facts Per Serving

- Calories: 149
- Fat: 12.9g
- Carb: 4.4g
- Protein: 5g

No-Dairy Cloud Bread

Prep time: 10 minutes
Cook time: 20 minutes
Servings: 6

Ingredients

- 4 egg yolks
- 4 egg whites
- ½ tsp. lemon juice
- 4 tbsp. mayonnaise
- ½ tsp. parsley
- ¼ tsp. garlic powder

Method

1. Preheat the oven to 400F.
2. Add egg whites and lemon juice into a bowl and beat with a hand mixer until stiff peaks form.
3. In another bowl, add mayo, egg yolks, garlic, and parsley and mix until combined for 1 minute.
4. Fold in the lemon juice mixture into the mayonnaise mixture in 3 to 4 sets.
5. Line baking sheets with parchment paper.
6. Add ¼ cup of the mixture onto the prepared baking pan until 12 even circles are formed.
7. Transfer baking sheets into the preheated oven and bake for 20 minutes.
8. Remove baking sheets from the oven and cool.
9. Serve.

Nutritional Facts Per Serving

- Calories: 110
- Fat: 10.25g
- Carb: 0.33g
- Protein: 3.72g

Almond Bread

Prep time: 10 minutes
Cook time: 30 minutes
Servings: 20

Ingredients

- 1 ½ cups almond flour
- 3 tsp. baking powder
- 4 tbsp. butter, melted
- ¼ tsp. cream of tartar
- 6 eggs, whites and yolks separated
- Pinch of salt

Method

1. Preheat the oven to 375F.
2. Grease a (8 x 4) inch loaf pan.
3. In a bowl, beat the cream of tartar and egg whites until soft peaks form.
4. Keep the mix on the side.
5. In a food processor, mix almond flour, salt, baking powder, egg yolks, and butter.
6. Add 1/3 cup egg whites to food processor and pulse until combined.
7. Add rest of the egg whites and mix until combined.
8. Pour into the prepared loaf pan and bake for 30 minutes.
9. Cool, slice, and serve.

Nutritional Facts Per Serving

- Calories: 271
- Fat: 22g
- Carb: 6g
- Protein: 5g

Tasty Psyllium Husk Bread

Prep time: 5 minutes
Cook time: 55 minutes
Servings: 15

Ingredients

- 6 tbsp. whole psyllium husks (finely ground)
- 1 cup coconut flour
- 8 egg whites
- ¾ tsp. sea salt
- ½ cup avocado oil
- 2 large eggs
- 1 ½ tsp. baking soda
- ¼ cup melted coconut oil
- ¾ cup warm water

Method

1. Preheat the oven to 350F.
2. Prepare a baking pan with parchment paper.
3. Add every ingredient into a food processor and process until combined.
4. Add batter into the prepared baking pan and spread until even at the top.
5. Transfer baking pan into the preheated oven and bake for 45 to 55 minutes, or until an inserted toothpick comes out clean and bread edges are browned.
6. Remove bread from the oven and cool for 15 minutes.
7. Serve.

Nutritional Facts Per Serving

- Calories: 127
- Fat: 13.3g
- Carb: 6g
- Protein: 3g

Cheese Garlic Bread

Prep time: 10 minutes
Cook time: 15 minutes
Servings: 10

Ingredients

- 2 cups mozzarella cheese, shredded
- 1 cup almond meal
- 1 tbsp. crushed garlic
- 2 tbsp. full fat cream cheese
- 1 tsp. baking powder
- 1 tbsp. dried parsley
- 1 medium egg
- 1 pinch salt

Method

1. Add every ingredient into a bowl, excluding the egg.
2. Lightly stir the mixture until combined.`
3. Place bowl in a microwave and microwave for 1 minute on high.
4. Stir mixture and microwave for 30 seconds more.
5. Add the egg into the dough and gently stir until incorporated.
6. Add mixture onto a prepared baking tray and mold into a loaf shape.
7. Sprinkle any leftover cheese over the bread.
8. Bake loaf for 15 minutes at 425F, or until golden brown.

Nutritional Facts Per Serving

- Calories: 117.4
- Fat: 9.8g
- Carb: 2.4g
- Protein: 6.2g

Pumpkin Bread

Prep time: 15 minutes

Cook time: 1 hour

Servings: 8

Ingredients

- 3 tbsp. walnuts, chopped
- 3 tbsp. pumpkin seeds plus extra for topping
- 2 eggs
- ¼ cup no-sugar-added apple sauce
- 2 tbsp. coconut oil
- ¾ cup pumpkin puree
- ½ tbsp. butter
- 1 tbsp. pumpkin pie spice
- ½ tbsp. baking powder
- ½ tsp. salt
- 1 tbsp. psyllium husk powder
- ¼ cup flaxseed
- ½ cup almond flour
- ½ cup coconut flour

Method

1. Preheat the oven to 400F. Grease a baking tray with butter.
2. Combine all the dry ingredients in a bowl except pumpkin seeds.
3. Whisk together apple sauce, eggs, pumpkin puree, and oil in another bowl.
4. Combine the dry mixture with the egg mixture.
5. Transfer the mixture to a baking tray and sprinkle with pumpkin seeds.
6. Place the tray on the lower rack of the oven. Bake for 1 hour.
7. Cool, slice, and serve.

Nutritional Facts Per Serving

- Calories: 194
- Fat: 13.8g
- Carb: 4.6g
- Protein: 6.3g

Rich Seed Bread

Prep time: 5 minutes
Cook time: 45 minutes
Servings: 20

Ingredients

- 1 cup almond flour
- ¾ cup coconut flour
- ½ cup flaxseed
- 5 1/3 tbsp. sesame seeds
- 3 tsp. baking powder
- ¼ cup psyllium husk powder
- 1 tsp. salt
- 1 tsp. ground fennel seeds
- 7 ounces cream cheese, room temp
- 6 eggs
- ¾ cup heavy whipping cream
- ½ cup melted butter
- 1 tbsp. poppy seeds

Method

1. Preheat the oven to 350F.
2. Excluding the poppy seeds, add all dry ingredients into a bowl. Mix well.
3. Add other ingredients into another bowl, excluding the poppy seeds and whisk until smooth.
4. Add the flour mixture into the melted butter mixture and mix well.
5. Transfer dough into a parchment paper lined loaf pan and spread evenly. Sprinkle with poppy seeds.
6. Place the loaf pan in the oven. Bake in the oven's lower rack for 45 minutes.
7. Remove, cool, slice, and serve.

Nutritional Facts Per Serving

- Calories: 223
- Fat: 20g
- Carb: 2g
- Protein: 6g

Herbed Garlic Bread

Prep time: 10 minutes
Cook time: 45 minutes
Servings: 10

Ingredients

- ½ cup coconut flour
- 8 tbsp. melted butter, cooled
- 1 tsp. baking powder
- 6 large eggs
- 1 tsp. garlic powder
- 2 tsp. rosemary, dried
- ¼ tsp. salt
- ½ tsp. onion powder

Method

1. Add coconut flour, baking powder, onion, garlic, rosemary, and salt into a bowl. Combine and mix well.
2. Add the eggs into another bowl and beat until bubbly on top.
3. Add melted butter into the bowl with the eggs and beat until mixed.
4. Gradually add the coconut flour mixture into the egg mixture. Mix with a hand mixer.
5. Preheat the oven to 350F.
6. Prepare a greased loaf pan.
7. Pour batter into the prepared loaf pan. Smooth the top with a spatula.
8. Transfer loaf pan into the preheated oven and bake for 40 to 50 minutes.
9. Cool, slice, and serve.

Nutritional Facts Per Serving

- Calories: 147
- Fat: 12.5g
- Carb: 3.5g
- Protein: 4.6g

Pita Bread

Prep time: 10 minutes
Cook time: 15 minutes
Servings: 8

Ingredients

- 2 cups almond flour, sifted
- ½ cup water
- 2 tbsp. olive oil
- Salt, to taste
- 1 tsp. black cumin

Method

1. Preheat the oven to 400F.
2. Combine the flour with salt. Add the water and olive oil.
3. Knead the dough and let stand for 15 minutes.
4. Shape the dough into 8 balls.
5. Line a baking sheet with parchment paper and flatten the balls into 8 thin rounds.
6. Sprinkle black cumin.
7. Bake for 15 minutes, serve.

Nutritional Facts Per Serving

- Calories: 73
- Fat: 6.9g
- Carb: 1.6g
- Protein: 1.6g

Multi-Purpose Bread

Prep time: 10 minutes
Cook time: 1 hour 30 minutes
Servings: 12

Ingredients

- ½ cup coconut flour
- 6 egg whites
- 2 whole eggs
- 1 ½ cup sesame seed flour
- 1/3 cup psyllium husk powder
- 1 tbsp. baking powder
- ½ to 1 tsp. salt
- 2 cups boiling water

Method

1. Preheat the oven to 350F.
2. Line a loaf pan with parchment paper. Set aside.
3. Whisk egg whites and whole eggs.
4. Combine dry ingredients and egg mix. Place in a mixer, and combine to make a thick dough.
5. Gradually pour in boiling water and mix well.
6. Transfer mix to prepared loaf pan and bake for 90 minutes.
7. Remove and cool.
8. Serve.

Nutritional Facts Per Serving

- Calories: 350
- Fat: 21g
- Carb: 9g
- Protein: 17g

5-Ingredient Bread

Prep time: 10 minutes
Cook time: 45 minutes
Servings: 6

Ingredients

- ¼ cup butter, melted
- 3 eggs
- ¾ cup almond flour
- ½ tsp. baking powder
- ½ tsp. Erythritol

Method

1. Layer a loaf pan with parchment paper and preheat the oven to 350F.
2. Whisk the eggs and melted butter in a bowl.
3. Mix erythritol, almond flour, and baking powder in another bowl.
4. Combine the two mixtures to form a dough.
5. Transfer the mixture to the loaf pan. Place it in the oven.
6. Bake for about 45 minutes and remove it from the oven.
7. Cool, slice, and serve.

Nutritional Facts Per Serving

- Calories: 184
- Fat: 16.5g
- Carb: 4.6g
- Protein: 5.9g

Cauliflower Garlic Bread

Prep time: 10 minutes
Cook time: 55 minutes
Servings: 6

Ingredients

- ½ medium head cauliflower, broken into florets and boiled
- 3 eggs, separated
- ½ cup almond flour
- ½ tbsp. parsley, chopped
- 3 cloves garlic, minced
- ½ tsp. basil, dried
- ½ tbsp. baking powder
- ¼ tbsp. salt

Method

1. Preheat the oven to 350F. Line a loaf pan with parchment paper.
2. Mash the prepared cauliflower in a bowl and add the baking powder, almond flour, egg yolks, parsley, basil, garlic, and salt.
3. Mix well and fold in the egg whites with a spatula.
4. Transfer the mixture into the loaf pan and bake for 55 minutes.
5. Cool, slice, and serve.

Nutritional Facts Per Serving

- Calories: 103
- Fat: 6.7g
- Carb: 5.8g
- Protein: 5.8g

Coconut Cauliflower Bread

Prep time: 20 minutes
Cook time: 45 minutes
Servings: 4

Ingredients

- 2 cups cauliflower rice
- 2 ½ tbsp. coconut flour
- 2 eggs, beaten
- 2 tbsp. garlic and onion spice blend
- ½ tbsp. psyllium husk powder
- ¼ tbsp. baking powder
- ½ tsp. salt

Method

1. Preheat the oven to 400F. Line a loaf pan with parchment paper.
2. Mix all the ingredients in a bowl and scoop the batter into the prepared baking pan.
3. Press down slightly and transfer into the oven.
4. Bake for 45 minutes.
5. Remove, slice, and serve.

Nutritional Facts Per Serving

- Calories: 67
- Fat: 2.7g
- Carb: 7.4g
- Protein: 4.4g

Flaxseed Bread

Prep time: 20 minutes
Cook time: 25 minutes
Servings: 6

Ingredients

- 1 cup flaxseed meal
- ½ tbsp. stevia powder
- ½ tbsp. baking powder
- ½ tbsp. Italian herb mix
- ½ tsp. salt
- 3 eggs, beaten
- ½ tbsp. olive oil
- ¼ cup water
- ¼ cup cottage cheese

Method

1. Preheat the oven to 350F. Line a baking pan with parchment paper.
2. Mix flaxseed meal, stevia powder, baking powder, salt, and Italian herb mix in a bowl.
3. In another bowl, whisk eggs with water, olive oil, and cottage cheese.
4. Combine the ingredients of both bowls and let the dough rest for 3 minutes.
5. Transfer the mixture to the baking pan.
6. Bake for 25 minutes.
7. Cool, slice, and serve.

Nutritional Facts Per Serving

- Calories: 150
- Fat: 9.5g
- Carb: 6g
- Protein: 7.6g

Coconut Zucchini Bread

Prep time: 20 minutes
Cook time: 40 minutes
Servings: 6

Ingredients

- ¼ cup zucchini, grated
- ½ cup coconut flour
- ½ tbsp. baking powder
- 1 scoop stevia
- 3 eggs
- ½ scoop protein powder
- ¼ cup butter
- ¼ tsp. salt

Method

1. Preheat the oven to 330F. Grease a loaf pan lightly.
2. Mix the coconut flour, protein powder, baking powder, and stevia in a bowl.
3. Whisk together eggs with zucchini and salt in a bowl.
4. Add the flour mixture to the egg mixture and combine well.
5. Pour batter into a loaf pan and transfer into the oven.
6. Bake for 40 minutes and remove it from the oven.
7. Serve hot.

Nutritional Facts Per Serving

- Calories: 151
- Fat: 11g
- Carb: 7.9g
- Protein: 6.1g

Low-Carb Holiday Bread

Prep time: 25 minutes
Cook time: 1 hour
Servings: 12

Ingredients

- 1 cup almond flour
- ¼ cup coconut flour
- 3 tbsp. sesame seeds
- 3 tbsp. flaxseed
- 2 tbsp. psyllium husk powder
- ½ tbsp. baking powder
- ½ tsp. salt
- 3 eggs
- ½ cup sour cream
- ¼ cup cream cheese
- 1 tbsp. cloves, ground
- ½ tbsp. bitter orange peel, ground
- ½ tbsp. fennel seeds
- 1 tsp. anise seeds
- 1 tsp. cardamom, ground

Method

1. Preheat the oven to 400F. Lightly grease a loaf pan.
2. Mix all the dry ingredients together in a bowl.
3. Whisk together eggs, sour cream, and cream cheese in another bowl.
4. Combine the dry mixture with the egg mixture and stir well.
5. Transfer the mixture to the loaf pan. Place in the oven.
6. Slice and serve.

Nutritional Facts Per Serving

- Calories: 85
- Fat: 6.6g
- Carb: 4g
- Protein: 2.9g

Puri Bread

Prep time: 10 minutes
Cook time: 5 minutes
Servings: 6

Ingredients

- 1 cup almond flour, sifted
- ½ cup of warm water
- 2 tbsp. clarified butter
- 1 cup olive oil for frying
- Salt to taste

Method

1. Salt the water and add the flour.
2. Make a hole in the center of the dough and pour warm clarified butter.
3. Knead the dough and let stand for 15 minutes, covered.
4. Shape into 6 balls.
5. Flatten the balls into 6 thin rounds using a rolling pin.
6. Heat enough oil to completely cover a round frying pan.
7. Place a puri in it when hot.
8. Fry for 20 seconds on each side.
9. Place on a paper towel.
10. Repeat with the rest of the puri and serve.

Nutritional Facts Per Serving

- Calories: 106
- Fat: 3g
- Carb: 6g
- Protein: 3g

Low-Carb Bread Loaf

Prep time: 10 minutes
Cook time: 45 minutes
Servings: 16

Ingredients

- 2/3 cup coconut flour
- ½ cup butter, melted
- 3 tbsp. coconut oil, melted
- 1 1/3 cups almond flour
- ½ tsp. xanthan gum
- 1 tsp. baking powder
- 6 eggs
- ½ tsp. salt

Method

1. Preheat the oven to 350F. Line a bread loaf pan with parchment paper.
2. Beat the eggs until creamy.
3. Add in the almond flour and coconut flour and mix them for 1 minute.
4. Now add the xanthan gum, coconut oil, butter, baking powder, and salt and mix them until the dough turns thick.
5. Put the dough into the prepared bread loaf pan.
6. Bake for 40 to 45 minutes.
7. Cool, slice, and serve.

Nutritional Facts Per Serving

- Calories: 174
- Fat: 15g
- Carb: 5g
- Protein: 5g

Cranberry Bread

Prep time: 10 minutes
Cook time: 1 hour 15 minutes
Servings: 12

Ingredients

- ½ cup coconut milk
- ½ tsp. baking soda
- ½ cup powdered Erythritol
- ½ tsp. powdered stevia
- ½ tsp. salt
- 1 bag (6-oz) cranberries
- 1 ½ tsp. baking powder
- 2 cups almond flour
- 4 eggs
- 4 tbsp. unsalted melted butter

Method

1. Preheat the oven to 350F. Line a loaf pan with parchment paper.
2. Add the flour, erythritol, baking powder, stevia, salt, and baking soda into a bowl and combine.
3. In another bowl, add in the butter, coconut milk, eggs, and mix well.
4. Combine the erythritol mixture with the butter mixture. Then add in the cranberries and fold them. Transfer into the loaf pan.
5. Bake in the oven for 1 hour and 15 minutes.
6. Cool, slice, and serve.

Nutritional Facts Per Serving

- Calories: 179
- Fat: 15g
- Carb: 7g
- Protein: 6.4g

Almond Cinnamon Bread

Prep time: 10 minutes
Cook time: 30 minutes
Servings: 9

Ingredients

- 2 cups almond flour
- 2 tbsp. coconut flour
- ½ tsp. sea salt
- 1 tsp. baking soda
- ¼ cup flax seed meal.
- 5 eggs plus 1 egg white, whisked
- 1 ½ tsp. juiced lime
- 2 tbsp. no-sugar-added maple syrup
- 3 tbsp. butter, divided and melted
- 1 tbsp. cinnamon plus extra for topping

Method

1. Preheat the oven to 350F. Line a loaf pan with parchment paper.
2. In a bowl, combine the almond flour, coconut flour, baking soda, salt, ½ tbsp. cinnamon, and flaxseed meal together.
3. In another bowl, add in the egg white and eggs and whisk together. Add in the maple syrup, butter, vinegar, and combine.
4. Pour the flour mixture into the egg mixture then mix to combine.
5. Transfer into the lined loaf pan.
6. Bake at 350F for 30 to 35 minutes. Remove.
7. Combine the remaining cinnamon and melted butter together then use it to rub the baked bread.
8. Cool, slice, and serve.

Nutritional Facts Per Serving

- Calories: 221
- Fat: 15.4g
- Carb: 10.7g
- Protein: 9.3g

Eggy Coconut Bread

Prep time: 10 minutes
Cook time: 40 minutes
Servings: 4

Ingredients

- ½ cup coconut flour
- 4 eggs
- 1 cup water
- 2 tbsp. apple cider vinegar
- ¼ cup coconut oil, plus 1 tsp. melted
- ½ tsp. garlic powder
- ½ tsp. baking soda
- ¼ tsp. salt

Method

1. Preheat the oven to 350F.
2. Grease a baking tin with 1 tsp. coconut oil. Set aside.
3. Add eggs to a blender along with vinegar, water, and ¼-cup coconut oil. Blend for 30 seconds.
4. Add coconut flour, baking soda, garlic powder, and salt. Blend for 1 minute.
5. Transfer to the baking tin.
6. Bake for 40 minutes.
7. Enjoy.

Nutritional Facts Per Serving

- Calories: 297
- Fat: 14g
- Carb: 9g
- Protein: 15g

Garlic & Rosemary Bread

Prep time: 10 minutes
Cook time: 45 minutes
Servings: 10

Ingredients

- ¼ tsp. pink Himalayan salt
- ½ cup coconut flour
- ½ tsp. powdered onion
- ½ tsp. powdered garlic
- 1 tsp. baking powder
- 2 tsp. dried rosemary
- 6 large eggs
- 8 tbsp. melted butter

Method

1. In a bowl, combine the baking powder, coconut flour, garlic, onion, salt, and rosemary.
2. Add the 6 eggs into another bowl, then whisk.
3. Gently add the melted butter into the egg mixture then beat again to combine.
4. Carefully add the baking powder mixture into the egg mixture then incorporate it together.
5. Grease a medium-sized loaf pan with cooking oil then empty the batter into the pan.
6. Bake in the oven for 40 to 50 minutes or until baked.
7. Cool, slice, and serve.

Nutritional Facts Per Serving

- Calories: 147
- Fat: 12.5g
- Carb: 3.5g
- Protein: 4.6g

Chocolate Zucchini Bread

Prep time: 10 minutes
Cook time: 20 minutes
Servings: 10

Ingredients

- 2 cups grated zucchini, excess moisture removed
- 4 eggs
- 2 tbsp. olive oil
- 1/3 cup low-carb sweetener
- 1 tsp. vanilla extract
- 1/3 cup coconut flour
- ¼ cup unsweetened cocoa powder
- ½ tsp. baking soda
- ½ tsp. salt
- 1/3 cup sugar-free chocolate chips

Method

1. Preheat the oven to 350F.
2. Grease the baking pan and line the entire pan with parchment paper.
3. In a food processor, blend the eggs, zucchini, oil, sweetener, and vanilla.
4. Add the cocoa, flour, baking soda, and salt to the zucchini mixture and stir until mixed. Let the batter sit for a few minutes.
5. Mix in the chocolate chips, then pour the batter into the prepared pan.
6. Bake for 45 to 50 minutes.
7. Cool, slice, and serve.

Nutritional Facts Per Serving

- Calories: 149
- Fat: 8g
- Carb: 7g
- Protein: 3g

Healthy Low Carb Bread

Prep time: 15 minutes
Cook time: 35 minutes
Servings: 8

Ingredients

- 2/3 cup coconut flour
- 2/3 cup coconut oil (softened not melted)
- 9 eggs
- 2 tsp. cream of tartar
- ¾ tsp. xanthan gum
- 1 tsp. baking soda
- ¼ tsp. salt

Method

1. Preheat the oven to 350F.
2. Grease a loaf pan with 1 to 2 tsp. melted coconut oil and place in the freezer to harden.
3. Add eggs into a bowl and mix for 2 minutes with a hand mixer.
4. Add coconut oil into the eggs and mix.
5. Add dry ingredients in a second bowl and whisk until mixed.
6. Add the dry ingredients into the egg mixture and mix on low speed with a hand mixer until dough is formed and the mixture is incorporated.
7. Add the dough into the prepared loaf pan, transfer into the preheated oven, and bake for 35 minutes.
8. Take out loaf pan from the oven.
9. Cool, slice, and serve.

Nutritional Facts Per Serving

- Calories: 229
- Fat: 25.5g
- Carb: 6.5g
- Protein: 8.5g

Delicious Bread

Prep time: 10 minutes
Cook time: 45 minutes
Servings: 12

Ingredients

- 2 cups almond flour
- ½ cup ghee, melted
- 7 large eggs
- 1 tsp. baking powder
- ¼ tsp. sea salt

Method

1. Preheat the oven to 350F.
2. Line a baking pan with parchment paper.
3. Beat eggs in a bowl on high speed with a hand mixer.
4. Add melted ghee into the bowl with the eggs and beat until mixed.
5. Beat on low speed and add every other ingredient into the bowl and beat until combined.
6. Add batter into the prepared pan and spread evenly.
7. Transfer loaf pan to the oven and bake for 40 to 45 minutes or until the top is just golden.
8. Cool, slice, and serve.

Nutritional Facts Per Serving

- Calories: 200
- Fat: 24g
- Carb: 3g
- Protein: 9g

Cinnamon Swirl Almond Bread

Prep time: 15 minutes
Cook time: 40 minutes
Servings: 16

Ingredients

- 2 ½ cups almond flour
- ¼ cup chopped walnuts
- ¼ cup melted coconut oil
- 4 eggs
- ½ cup hot water
- ½ cup Erythritol
- 1 tbsp. cinnamon + 2 tsp.
- ½ tsp. salt
- 1 tsp. baking powder
- 4 tbsp. psyllium husk

Method

1. Preheat the oven to 375F.
2. In a bowl, mix erythritol, 1 tbsp. cinnamon, salt, baking powder, psyllium husk, and almond flour.
3. Add hot water and mix well.
4. Add coconut oil and eggs and mix.
5. Grease an 8-inch bread pan and pour half the batter.
6. Sprinkle 2 tsp. cinnamon on top.
7. Pour the remaining batter into the pan.
8. Make a swirl with a knife.
9. Sprinkle with chopped walnuts.
10. Bake in the oven for 40 minutes.
11. Serve.

Nutritional Facts Per Serving

- Calories: 166
- Fat: 14g
- Carb: 7g
- Protein: 5g

Almond Sweet Bread

Prep time: 10 minutes
Cook time: 50 minutes
Servings: 14

Ingredients

- 2 ¼ cup almond flour
- 2 eggs
- 2 tbsp. ground flaxseed
- ¼ tsp. ground star anise
- ¼ tsp. ginger powder
- 1 tsp. baking powder
- ½ tsp. xanthan gum
- ½ cup heavy cream
- ½ cup sugar substitute
- ½ cup butter

Method

1. Melt the butter in a pan. Add heavy cream and sugar substitute. Stir until mixed well. Remove from the heat and cool.
2. Place the rest of the dry ingredients in a bowl and whisk. Pour in the cooled cream and butter mix. Add 2 eggs and mix.
3. Line a bread in with parchment paper and pour the bread dough.
4. Bake at 350F for 45 to 50 minutes.
5. Remove, cool, and serve.

Nutritional Facts Per Serving

- Calories: 206
- Fat: 19.8g
- Carb: 2.3g
- Protein: 5.2g

Best Diabetic Bread

Prep time: 10 minutes
Cook time: 30 minutes
Servings: 20

Ingredients

- 1 ½ cup almond flour
- 6 drops liquid stevia
- 1 pinch Pink Himalayan salt
- ¼ tsp. cream of tartar
- 3 tsp. baking powder
- ¼ cup butter, melted
- 6 large eggs, separated

Method

1. Preheat the oven to 375F.
2. To the egg whites, add cream of tartar and beat until soft peaks are formed.
3. In a food processor, combine stevia, salt, baking powder, almond flour, melted butter, 1/3 of the beaten egg whites, and egg yolks. Mix well.
4. Then add the remaining 2/3 of the egg whites and gently process until fully mixed. Don't over mix.
5. Grease a (8 x 4) loaf pan and pour the mixture in it.
6. Bake for 30 minutes.
7. Enjoy.

Nutritional Facts Per Serving

- Calories: 90
- Fat: 7g
- Carb: 2g
- Protein: 3g

Paleo Coconut Bread

Prep time: 10 minutes
Cook time: 50 minutes
Servings: 10

Ingredients

- ½ cup coconut flour
- ¼ cup almond milk (unsweetened)
- ¼ cup coconut oil (melted)
- 6 eggs
- ¼ tsp. baking soda
- ¼ tsp. salt

Method

1. Preheat the oven to 350F.
2. Line an (8 x 4) loaf pan with parchment paper.
3. In a bowl, combine salt, baking soda, and coconut flour.
4. Combine the oil, milk, and eggs in another bowl.
5. Gradually add the wet ingredients into the dry ingredients and mix well.
6. Pour the mixture into the prepared loaf pan.
7. Bake for 40 to 50 minutes.
8. Cool, slice and serve.

Nutritional Facts Per Serving

- Calories: 108
- Fat: 8.7g
- Carb: 3.4g
- Protein: 4.2g

Iranian Flatbread

Prep time: 3 hours 15 minutes
Cook time: 6 minutes
Servings: 6

Ingredients

- 4 cups almond flour
- 2 ½ cups warm water
- 1 tbsp. instant yeast
- 12 tsp. sesame seeds
- Salt to taste

Method

1. In a bowl, add 1 Tbsp. yeast to ½ cup warm water. Let stand for 5 minutes to activate.
2. Add salt and 1 cup water. Let stand for 10 minutes more.
3. Add flour 1 cup at a time. Then add the remaining water.
4. Knead the dough and then shape into a ball and let stand for 3 hours covered.
5. Preheat the oven to 480F.
6. With a rolling pin, roll out the dough and divide into 6 balls. Roll each ball into ½ inch thick rounds.
7. Line a baking sheet with parchment paper. Place the rolled rounds on it. With a finger, make a small hole in the middle and add 2 tsp. sesame seeds in each hole.
8. Bake for 3 to 4 minutes and then flip over and bake for 2 minutes more.

Nutritional Facts Per Serving

- Calories: 26
- Fat: 1g
- Carb: 3.5g
- Protein: 1g

Blueberry Bread

Prep time: 15 minutes
Cook time: 1 hour 10 minutes
Servings: 12

Ingredients

- 10 tbsp. coconut flour
- 1 ½ tsp. baking powder
- ½ tsp. salt
- 2 tbsp. heavy whipping cream
- 1 ½ tsp. vanilla
- 2/3 cup Monkfruit classic
- 2 tbsp. sour cream
- ½ tsp. cinnamon
- ¾ cup fresh blueberries
- 9 tbsp. melted butter
- 6 eggs

For the icing

- ¼ tsp. lemon zest
- 1 tbsp. heavy whipping cream
- Dash of vanilla
- 1 tsp. butter (melted)
- 2 tbsp. Monkfruit powdered

Method

1. Line a regular loaf pan with parchment paper and preheat oven to 350F.
2. Melt butter.
3. Beat eggs, cinnamon, baking powder, salt, vanilla, whipping cream, sour cream, and Monkfruit until combined.
4. Add melted butter and mix well.
5. Add coconut flour and mix well.
6. Add a small amount of batter in the loaf pan and sprinkle with a couple of blueberries. Then spread more batter and sprinkle blueberries on top. Repeat to finish the batter and blueberries.
7. Bake for 65 to 75 minutes. Cool.
8. For the icing, combine all ingredients and whisk.
9. Drizzle over warm bread and serve.

Nutritional Facts Per Serving

- Calories: 155
- Fat: 13g
- Carb: 4g
- Protein: 3g

CHAPTER 3 SUGAR FREE MUFFINS AND BROWNIES

Almonds Pumpkin Muffins

Prep time: 10 minutes
Cook time: 18 minutes
Servings: 5

Ingredients

- ½ tsp. salt
- ½ tsp. baking powder
- 1 egg
- 1 tbsp. vanilla extract
- 1 tbsp. apple cider vinegar
- ½ cup pumpkin puree
- 2 tbsp. coconut oil
- ¼ cup sugar-free caramel syrup
- ¼ cup crushed almonds

Method

1. Preheat the oven to 350F.
2. Combine all of the components in the recipe list except for the almonds.
3. Prepare a muffin pan for 5 portions and spritz with oil.
4. Cover with crushed almonds.
5. Bake for 15 to 18 minutes.

Nutritional Facts Per Serving

- Calories: 185
- Fat: 13.5g
- Carb: 3.5g
- Protein: 7.4g

English Muffin

Prep time: 10 minutes
Cook time: 5 minutes
Servings: 2

Ingredients

- ¼ cup almond flour
- 1 tbsp. coconut flour
- 1/8 tsp. baking soda
- 1/8 tsp. salt
- 1 egg white
- ½ tsp. oil
- 2 tbsp. warm water
- Butter, jam, or scrambled egg for serving

Method

1. Add the flours, baking soda, and salt in a small ramekin and mix well with a fork.
2. Add the egg white, oil, and water, mix well.
3. Flatten the batter, so it is even on top.
4. Microwave the ramekin for 2 minutes.
5. Turn the ramekin upside down to slide out the muffin.
6. Slice it into 2 muffin halves and toast each slice.
7. Spread with butter or sugar-free jam or scrambled egg.
8. Serve.

Nutritional Facts Per Serving

- Calories: 114
- Fat: 1g
- Carb: 5g
- Protein: 5g

Chocolate Chip Muffins

Prep time: 10 minutes
Cook time: 20 minutes
Servings: 8

Ingredients

- ½ cup coconut flour
- ¼ tsp. baking soda
- ¼ tsp. salt
- 4 eggs
- 1/3 cup unsalted butter, melted
- ½ cup low-carb sweetener
- 1 tbsp. vanilla extract
- 2 tbsp. coconut milk
- 1/3 cup sugar-free chocolate chips

Method

1. Preheat the oven to 350F.
2. Add the coconut flour, baking soda, and salt in a bowl and blend well.
3. Add the butter, eggs, sweetener, vanilla, and coconut milk to the dry ingredients and mix well. Gently stir in the chocolate chips.
4. Line muffin tins and fill ¾.
5. Bake for 20 minutes.
6. Cool and serve.

Nutritional Facts Per Serving

- Calories: 168
- Fat: 13g
- Carb: 6g
- Protein: 5g

Blueberry Muffins

Prep time: 10 minutes
Cook time: 20 minutes
Servings: 12

Ingredients

- ½ cup granulated sweetener Swerve
- 2 ½ cup almond flour
- ½ tsp. vanilla extract
- ¾ cup blueberries
- 1 ½ tsp. baking powder
- 1/3 cup almond milk, unsweetened
- 3 eggs
- ¼ tsp. salt
- 1/3 cup coconut oil, solid

Method

1. Preheat the oven to 350F. Line a cupcake pan with baking paper liners.
2. Mix the almond flour, baking powder, salt, and sweetener in a bowl.
3. Heat the coconut oil in a saucepan. Then put it slowly to the mixture of flour when melted.
4. Then mix the eggs, almond milk, and vanilla into the batter and mix.
5. Fold in the blueberries into the mixture.
6. Distribute the batter to the muffin cups.
7. Bake for 20 minutes.
8. Serve.

Nutritional Facts Per Serving

- Calories: 125
- Fat: 15g
- Carb: 4g
- Protein: 6g

Brownies

Prep time: 10 minutes
Cook time: 20 minutes
Servings: 12

Ingredients

- 6 ounces coconut oil, melted
- 6 eggs
- 3 ounces of cocoa powder
- 2 tsp. vanilla extract
- ½ tsp. baking powder
- 4 ounces cream cheese
- 5 tbsp. Swerve

Method

1. In a bowl, mix eggs with coconut oil, cocoa powder, baking powder, vanilla extract, cream cheese, Swerve, and stir using a mixer.
2. Pour into a lined baking dish.
3. Place in an oven at 350F. Bake for 20 minutes.
4. Cool then slice into rectangle pieces.
5. Serve.

Nutritional Facts Per Serving

- Calories: 202
- Fat: 20.6g
- Carb: 4.3g
- Protein: 4.1g

Pumpkin Pie Cupcakes

Prep time: 15 minutes
Cook time: 30 minutes
Servings: 6

Ingredients

- 3 tbsp. coconut flour
- 1 tsp. pumpkin pie spice
- ¼ tsp. baking powder
- ¼ tsp. baking soda
- Pinch of salt
- ¾ cup pumpkin puree
- 1/3 cup Swerve
- ¼ cup heavy whipping cream
- 1 egg
- ½ tsp. vanilla

Method

1. Line 6 muffin cups with parchment paper and preheat the oven to 350F.
2. In a bowl, whisk together the salt, baking soda, baking powder, pumpkin pie spice, and coconut flour.
3. In another bowl, whisk egg, vanilla, cream, sweetener, and pumpkin puree until mixed. Whisk in dry ingredients.
4. Pour into the muffin cups. Bake until just puffed and almost set, about 25 to 30 minutes.
5. Remove and cool.
6. Refrigerate for about 1 hour.
7. Top with whipped cream and serve.

Nutritional Facts Per Serving

- Calories: 70
- Fat: 4.1g
- Carb: 5.1g
- Protein: 1.7g

CHAPTER 4 DIABETIC COOKIES

Shortbread Tart Cookies

Prep time: 20 minutes
Cook time: 15 minutes
Servings: 16

Ingredients

- 6 tbsp. butter
- 2 cups almond flour
- 1/3 cup granulated sweetener
- 1 tsp. freshly grated lemon zest

Method

1. In a small saucepan, melt the butter. Add the lemon zest, sweetener, and almond flour. Stir until combine fully.
2. To make the cookies: form a crumb dough into a cylinder.
3. Then wrap tightly with plastic wrap to compress.
4. Chill in the refrigerator for 2 hours or until firm.
5. Slice into ½-inch thick cookies with a knife.
6. Place them on a parchment-lined cookie sheet.
7. Bake in the oven at 350F until firm and golden brown, about 15 minutes.
8. Cool before removing.

Nutritional Facts Per Serving

- Calories: 119
- Fat: 11g
- Carb: 1.6g
- Protein: 3g

Coconut Cookies

Prep time: 10 minutes
Cook time: 7 minutes
Servings: 12

Ingredients

- 2 egg whites
- 1 ½ cups coconut flakes
- 2 oz. butter, melted, cooled
- 2 tbsp. coconut flour
- ¼ cup Erythritol

Method

1. Combine flour, coconut flakes, and erythritol.
2. Add egg whites and melted butter. Mix.
3. Line a baking sheet with parchment paper. Put the cookie batter on it by the spoonful.
4. Bake at 350F for 7 minutes.
5. Enjoy.

Nutritional Facts Per Serving

- Calories: 144
- Fat: 10.4g
- Carb: 7g
- Protein: 1.4g

Cream Cheese Cookies

Prep time: 10 minutes
Cook time: 15 minutes
Servings: 10

Ingredients

- 1 egg white
- ¼ cup butter, soft
- 3 cups almond flour
- 2 oz. cream cheese
- 2 tsp. vanilla extract
- ½ cup Erythritol

Method

1. Beat together the butter, cream cheese, and erythritol.
2. Add vanilla and egg white.
3. Gradually sift flour, ½ cup at a time into the mixture.
4. Line a baking sheet with parchment paper. Spoon the cookies onto it.
5. Bake at 350F for 15 minutes.
6. Serve.

Nutritional Facts Per Serving

- Calories: 106
- Fat: 9g
- Carb: 3g
- Protein: 3g

Chocolate Macaroon Cookie with Coconut

Prep time: 10 minutes
Cook time: 20 minutes
Servings: 20

Ingredients

- 1 cup almond flour
- 3 tbsp. coconut flour
- ¼ cup cocoa powder
- ½ tsp. baking powder
- 1/3 cup Erythritol
- 1/3 cup unsweetened coconut, shredded
- ¼ tsp. salt
- 2 eggs
- ¼ cup coconut oil
- 1 tsp. vanilla extract

Method

1. Combine all the dry ingredients. Add the wet ingredients and mix well.
2. Roll the dough into small balls.
3. Line a baking sheet with parchment paper. Place the cookie balls on a sheet.
4. Bake at 350F for 15 to 20 minutes.
5. Sprinkle with shredded coconut and serve.

Nutritional Facts Per Serving

- Calories: 77
- Fat: 7g
- Carb: 1g
- Protein: 2.2g

Chocolate Biscotti

Prep time: 10 minutes
Cook time: 12 minutes
Servings: 8

Ingredients

- 2 tbsp. chia seeds
- 2 cup almonds
- 1 egg
- ¼ cup of coconut oil
- ¼ cup coconut, shredded
- 2 tbsp. stevia
- ¼ cup of cocoa powder
- A pinch of salt
- 1 tsp. baking soda

Method

1. In a food processor, mix chia seeds with almonds and blend well.
2. Add egg, coconut, coconut oil, cocoa powder, salt, baking soda, and stevia and blend well.
3. Shape 8 biscotti pieces out of this dough.
4. Place on a lined baking sheet.
5. Bake in the oven at 350F for 12 minutes.

Nutritional Facts Per Serving

- Calories: 200
- Fat: 2g
- Carb: 3g
- Protein: 4g

Lemon and Coconut Cookies

Prep time: 10 minutes
Cook time: 15 minutes
Servings: 24

Ingredients

- 1 cup butter, softened
- ½ cup granulated sugar substitute
- 1 ½ cups coconut flour
- 4 eggs
- ½ tsp. salt
- ¼ cup chopped almonds
- 2 tsp. lemon extract

Method

1. Preheat the oven to 375F.
2. Line two cookie sheets with parchment paper.
3. In a bowl, combine the sugar substitute, lemon extract, salt, and butter and beat well together.
4. Add the eggs one at a time. Beating well after each addition.
5. Stir in the coconut flour.
6. Drop spoonfuls of the mix onto the prepared sheets, flatten with a fork.
7. Top with a sprinkle of chopped almonds and bake for 12 to 15 minutes.
8. Turn the cookies after 8 minutes to brown evenly.
9. Remove and serve.

Nutritional Facts Per Serving

- Calories: 118
- Fat: 9.6g
- Carb: 4.7g
- Protein: 2.2g

Chocolate Filled Peanut Butter Cookies

Prep time: 10 minutes
Cook time: 15 minutes
Servings: 20

Ingredients

- 2 ½ cups almond flour
- ½ cup peanut butter
- ¼ cup coconut oil
- ¼ cup Erythritol
- 3 tbsp. maple syrup
- 1 tbsp. vanilla extract
- 1 ½ tsp. baking powder
- ½ tsp. salt
- 2 to 3 dark chocolate bars

Method

1. Whisk the wet ingredients together.
2. Separately, mix the dry ingredients. Sift them into the wet ingredients and mix. Refrigerate for 20 to 30 minutes.
3. Break the dark chocolate bars into small squares.
4. From small balls of dough and press flat.
5. Add 1 to 2 pieces of chocolate in the middle and seal together into a ball.
6. Place on a parchment-paper-lined cookie tray and bake at 350F for 15 minutes.

Nutritional Facts Per Serving

- Calories: 150
- Fat: 14g
- Carb: 2.7g
- Protein: 4.5g

Butter Pecan Cookies

Prep time: 10 minutes
Cook time: 18 minutes
Servings: 20

Ingredients

- ½ cup unsalted butter, softened
- ½ cup Swerve sweetener
- 1 ¾ cup almond flour
- 2 tbsp. coconut flour
- ½ tsp. vanilla extract
- ½ tsp. salt
- ½ cup toasted and chopped pecans

Method

1. Line two rimmed baking sheets with parchment paper. Preheat the oven to 325F.
2. Beat sweetener and butter in a bowl for 2 minutes, or until fluffy.
3. Beat in salt, vanilla extract, coconut flour, and almond flour until mixed. Stir in chopped pecans.
4. Make 1-inch balls from the dough. Then place on the prepared baking sheets. Flatten them slightly with your hands.
5. Bake for 5 minutes. Remove from the oven and flatten them again at the bottom of a glass (about ¼ inch thick).
6. Bake again until edges are golden brown, about 10 to 12 minutes.
7. Remove, cool, and serve.

Nutritional Facts Per Serving

- Calories: 240
- Carb: 5.3g
- Fat: 22.3g
- Protein: 5g

Chocolate Cookies

Prep time: 10 minutes
Cook time: 40 minutes
Servings: 12

Ingredients

- 1 tsp. vanilla extract
- ½ cup ghee
- 1 egg
- 2 tbsp. Erythritol, powdered
- ¼ cup Swerve
- A pinch of salt
- 2 cups almond flour
- ½ cup chocolate chips, unsweetened

Method

1. Heat a pan with ghee over medium heat. Stir and cook until it browns.
2. Take this off the heat and leave aside for 5 minutes.
3. In a bowl, mix the egg with vanilla extract, erythritol, and Swerve and stir.
4. Add melted ghee, salt, flour, and half of the chocolate chips, and stir everything.
5. Transfer this to a pan; spread the remaining chocolate chips on top.
6. Bake in the oven at 350F for 30 minutes.
7. Slice when cold and serve.

Nutritional Facts Per Serving

- Calories: 230
- Fat: 12g
- Carb: 4g
- Protein: 5g

Shortbread Vanilla Cookies

Prep time: 15 minutes
Cook time: 20 minutes
Servings: 16

Ingredients

- 1 egg
- ½ cup unsalted butter, softened
- 1 tsp. vanilla extract
- 1 pinch salt
- 1/3 cup Erythritol
- 2 cups almond flour

Method

1. Preheat the oven to 300F.
2. Mix together the almond flour, erythritol, salt, and vanilla extract in a bowl.
3. Pour in butter and mix with the almond flour mix unit well combined. Add egg and mix well.
4. Roll one tbsp. mixture into a ball. Place them onto a lined cookie sheet with gaps in between. Press.
5. Place in the oven and bake for 12 to 25 minutes, or until the edges are browned.
6. Cool and serve.

Nutritional Facts Per Serving

- Calories: 126
- Fat: 12g
- Carb: 2g
- Protein: 3g

CHAPTER 5 DIABETIC BREADSTICKS

Cheesy Breadsticks

Prep time: 10 minutes
Cook time: 20 minutes
Servings: 5

Ingredients

- 2 cups shredded mozzarella cheese
- 2 tbsp. coconut flour
- 2 whole eggs
- 1 pinch of salt

Toppings

- ½ cup shredded parmesan cheese
- 1 tbsp. Italian seasoning
- ½ tsp. garlic powder

Method

1. Preheat the oven to 350F.
2. Line a baking sheet with parchment paper.
3. Add salt, eggs, coconut flour, and mozzarella to the food processor.
4. Process until smooth.
5. Scoop mix onto the lined baking sheet and flatten to 1-inch thickness, forming a square.
6. Bake for 15 minutes.
7. Remove from the oven. Sprinkle with parmesan cheese, garlic powder, and Italian seasoning.
8. Remove from the oven and let sticks cool for 10 to 15 minutes.
9. Slice and serve.

Nutritional Facts Per Serving

- Calories: 225
- Fat: 19g
- Carb: 2g
- Protein: 12g

Cauliflower Breadsticks

Prep time: 10 minutes
Cook time: 35 minutes
Servings: 8

Ingredients

- 2 cups riced cauliflower
- 1 cup mozzarella, shredded
- 1 tsp. Italian seasoning
- 2 eggs
- ½ tsp. ground pepper
- 1 tsp. salt
- ½ tsp. granulated garlic
- ¼ cup Parmesan cheese as a topping

Method

1. Preheat the oven to 350F. Grease a baking sheet.
2. Beat the eggs until mixed well.
3. Combine riced cauliflower, mozzarella cheese, Italian seasoning, pepper, garlic, and salt and blend on low speed in a food processor. Combine with eggs.
4. Pour the dough into the prepared cookie sheet and pat the dough down to ¼ thick across the pan.
5. Bake for 30 minutes and dust the breadsticks with the parmesan cheese.
6. Put the breadsticks on the broil setting for 2 to 3 minutes, so the cheese melts.
7. Slice and serve.

Nutritional Facts Per Serving

- Calories: 165
- Fat: 10g
- Carb: 5g
- Protein: 13g

Garlic-Cauliflower Breadsticks

Prep time: 10 minutes
Cook time: 20 minutes
Servings: 16

Ingredients

- 2 cups grated cauliflower, riced
- ½ cup grated Parmesan cheese, divided
- 1 garlic clove, minced
- ¼ tsp. salt
- 2 tsp. chopped fresh herb
- 1 egg
- 2 tbsp. coconut flour
- ½ cup marinara sauce

Method

1. Preheat the oven to 450F. Line a baking sheet with parchment paper.
2. Steam the riced cauliflower for 5 minutes or until tender, but not soft.
3. Remove excess moisture from the steamed cauliflower with cheesecloth.
4. Add the cauliflower, ¼ cup cheese, garlic, salt, herbs, egg, and coconut flour in a bowl and mix well.
5. On parchment paper, shape the mixture into a rectangle about ½ inch thick.
6. Bake the breadsticks for 15 minutes, or until the edges begin to brown.
7. Brush the top with marinara sauce and sprinkle the remaining ¼-cup cheese.
8. Place back in the oven and bake until the cheese starts to brown.
9. Cool, slice, and serve.

Nutritional Facts Per Serving

- Calories: 63
- Fat: 4g
- Carb: 1g
- Protein: 5g

Italian Breadsticks

Prep time: 10 minutes
Cook time: 15 minutes
Servings: 6

Ingredients

- 1 tbsp. pulverized psyllium husk
- ¾ cup almond flour
- 1 tbsp. flaxseed meal
- 3 tbsp. cream cheese
- 1 tsp. baking powder
- 2 cups mozzarella cheese, shredded
- 2 eggs
- 1 tsp. pepper
- 2 tsp. Italian seasoning
- 1 tsp. salt

Method

1. Preheat the oven to 400F. Line a baking sheet with baking paper.
2. Melt the mozzarella cheese completely with a double boiler.
3. Meanwhile, in another bowl, combine the eggs and cream cheese until mixed well. Set aside.
4. Whisk the psyllium husk, flaxseed meal, baking powder and almond flour in a bowl.
5. Add in the mixture of cheese to the bowl of dry ingredients and mix well. Next, add the melted mozzarella cheese to the batter.
6. Knead the dough by hand until thick.
7. Use a rolling pin to press the dough flat on parchment paper.
8. Transfer the flattened dough to another piece of parchment paper and cut it into strips with a pizza cutter.
9. Sprinkle the salt, Italian seasoning, and pepper on each breadstick.
10. Place on the baking sheet. Bake for 13 to 15 minutes.
11. Serve.

Nutritional Facts Per Serving

- Calories: 238
- Fat: 19g
- Carb: 2.8g
- Protein: 13g

Garlic Breadsticks

Prep time: 10 minutes
Cook time: 20 minutes
Servings: 8

Ingredients for the garlic butter

- ¼ cup butter, softened
- 1 tsp. garlic powder

Other ingredients

- 2 cups almond flour
- ½ tbsp. baking powder
- 1 tbsp. psyllium husk powder
- ¼ tsp. salt
- 3 tbsp. butter, melted
- 1 egg
- ¼ cup boiling water

Method

1. Preheat the oven to 400F. Line baking sheet with parchment paper.
2. Beat the butter with garlic powder and set aside to use it for brushing.
3. Combine the salt, psyllium husk powder, baking powder, and almond flour. Add the butter along with the egg. Mix until well combined.
4. Pour in the boiling water, mix until dough forms.
5. Divide the dough into 8 equal pieces. Roll them into breadsticks.
6. Place in the baking sheet and bake for 15 minutes.
7. Brush the breadsticks with the garlic butter and bake for 5 minutes more.
8. Serve.

Nutritional Facts Per Serving

- Calories: 259.2
- Fat: 24.7g
- Carb: 6.3g
- Protein: 7g

Diabetic-Bread Twists

Prep time: 20 minutes
Cook time: 20 minutes
Servings: 6

Ingredients

- ¼ cup almond flour
- 2 tbsp. coconut flour
- ½ tsp. salt
- ½ tbsp. baking powder
- ½ cup cheese, shredded
- 2 tbsp. butter
- 2 eggs
- ¼ cup green pesto

Method

1. Preheat the oven to 350F. Prepare a baking tray.
2. Combine coconut flour, almond flour, baking powder, and salt in a bowl.
3. Mix butter, cheese, and egg in another bowl.
4. Combine the flour mixture with the butter mixture and form a dough.
5. Take 2 parchment sheets and place the dough in between them.
6. Form the dough into a rectangular shape with a rolling pin and remove the parchment paper from one side.
7. Drizzle the green pesto on the loaf and cut it into strips and twist them.
8. Put the baking tray in the oven. Bake for 20 minutes.
9. Remove from oven and serve.

Nutritional Facts Per Serving

- Calories: 151
- Fat: 12.9g
- Carb: 3.5g
- Protein: 5.8g

Diabetic Breadsticks

Prep time: 10 minutes
Cook time: 10 minutes
Servings: 8

Ingredients

- 1/3 cup coconut flour
- 1/3 cup arrowroot flour
- ½ tsp. baking soda
- 1 ½ tsp. lemon juice
- 1 tsp. dried rosemary
- 3 tbsp. water
- 1 egg
- 4 tbsp. extra virgin olive oil, divided
- 1/8 tsp. garlic powder for topping
- 1/8 tsp. sea salt for topping

Method

1. Preheat the oven to 350F.
2. Line a baking sheet with parchment paper. Set aside.
3. Add all the ingredients to the food processor and pulse until well combined and the dough is formed.
4. Divide the dough into 8 equal balls. Roll them into breadsticks.
5. Arrange on the prepared sheet, brush with olive oil, and sprinkle with garlic powder and salt.
6. Bake for 10 minutes.

Nutritional Facts Per Serving

- Calories: 216
- Fat: 15.8g
- Carb: 8.1g
- Protein: 3.1g

Breadsticks

Prep time: 5 minutes
Cook time: 15 minutes
Servings: 10

Ingredients

- 2 eggs
- 1 ½ tbsp. olive oil
- ½ tsp. oregano
- ½ tsp. parsley
- ½ tsp. basil
- ½ tsp. garlic powder
- ½ tsp. onion powder
- 2 ½ tbsp. coconut flour
- 2 cups almond flour

Topping

- ¼ tsp. salt
- ½ tsp. garlic powder
- 2 tsp. parmesan grated
- 1 tbsp. olive oil

Method

1. Preheat the oven to 350F. Line a baking pan with parchment paper.
2. In a bowl, whisk almond flour, olive oil, and seasoning.
3. Whisk the eggs in another bowl, mix into the almond flour.
4. Add 1 tbsp. coconut flour to the mixture at a time, stirring to combine.
5. Allow dough to rest for 1 to 2 minutes after each tbsp. Once the mixture gets thick, add the remaining coconut flour.
6. Form dough into a ball, about 2 tbsp. and roll out into 1.5-inch wide rope-like sticks.
7. Transfer to the prepared baking sheet. Place in the oven, bake for 10 minutes.
8. Meanwhile, mix together salt, parmesan, and garlic.
9. Once baked, carefully brush the tops of breadsticks with oil, then sprinkle with garlic parmesan mix.
10. Bake for 5 minutes more.

Nutritional Facts Per Serving:

- Calories: 169
- Fat: 15.15g
- Carb: 6.14g
- Protein: 6.65g

Ultimate Sugar-Free Breadsticks

Prep time: 10 minutes
Cook time: 20 minutes
Servings: 20

Ingredients

- ¼ cup coconut flour
- ¾ cup ground flax seeds
- 1 tbsp. psyllium husk powder
- 1 cup almond flour
- 2 tbsp. ground chia seeds
- 1 tsp. salt
- 1 cup lukewarm water, plus more if needed

Ingredients for the topping

- 2 egg yolks, for brushing
- 4 tbsp. mixed seeds
- 1 tsp. coarse sea salt

Method

1. Combine the almond flour, psyllium husks, flax seeds, and coconut flour. Add the chia seeds, salt, and the water. Mix until dough is formed. Refrigerate for 20 minutes.
2. Preheat the oven to 350F. Line a baking sheet with parchment paper.
3. Divide the dough into 20 equal pieces. Roll them with your hands forming breadsticks.
4. Arrange the breadsticks on the baking sheet and brush them with the egg yolks.
5. Sprinkle with seeds and salt and bake for 20 minutes.
6. Serve.

Nutritional Facts Per Serving

- Calories: 75.2
- Fat: 9.6g
- Carb: 4.1g
- Protein: 3.5g

CHAPTER 6 BAGEL RECIPES

Low-Carb Bagels

Prep time: 15 minutes
Cook time: 30 minutes
Servings: 8

Ingredients

- ½ cup almond flour
- ¼ cup coconut flour
- ½ tbsp. psyllium husk
- 1 egg
- 1 egg white
- 2 tbsp. coconut oil
- 2 tbsp. coconut milk
- ½ tbsp. apple cider vinegar
- ¼ cup boiling water

Method

1. Preheat the oven to 375F. Line a baking sheet with parchment paper.
2. Whisk together the egg, egg white, apple cider vinegar, coconut milk, and coconut oil in a bowl.
3. Sift the rest of the ingredients in another bowl through a sieve.
4. Combine the two mixtures with a spatula and add boiling water.
5. Wet your hands and roll the dough into 8 even balls.
6. Transfer the balls onto the baking sheet and flatten the dough to make the typical bagel shapes.
7. Place the sheet in the oven. Bake for 30 minutes.
8. Cool and serve.

Nutritional Facts Per Serving

- Calories: 110
- Fat: 8.6g
- Carb: 6.4g
- Protein: 3.2g

Buttery Bagels

Prep time: 10 minutes
Cook time: 23 minutes
Servings: 6

Ingredients

- ½ tsp. baking soda
- 1 ¾ tbsp. butter, unsalted and melted
- 3 eggs, separated
- ¼ tsp. cream of tartar
- 2 tbsp. coconut flour, sifted
- 1 ¾ tbsp. cream cheese, full-fat and softened
- 2 tsp. Swerve sweetener, granulated
- ¼ tsp. salt
- Coconut oil cooking spray

Method

1. Preheat the oven to 300F. Coat a 6-cavity donut pan with coconut oil spray.
2. Divide the eggs between whites and yolks.
3. Blend the cream of tartar with the egg whites and pulse with a hand mixer for 5 minutes.
4. Combine the egg yolks with salt, baking soda, Swerve, coconut flour, melted butter, and cream cheese.
5. Gently blend the whipped eggs into the mix and blend well.
6. Fill the pan with the batter.
7. Bake in the oven for 23 minutes.
8. Cool and serve.

Nutritional Facts Per Serving

- Calories: 83
- Fat: 3g
- Carb: 1.2g
- Protein: 6g

Easy Cheese Bagel

Prep time: 2 minutes
Cook time: 15 minutes
Servings: 6

Ingredients

- 1 cup cheese, any kind, shredded
- ½ cup grated parmesan, grated
- 2 eggs
- 2 tbsp. bagel seasoning

Method

1. Preheat the oven to 375F.
2. In a bowl, combine egg and both kinds of cheese and mix to combine.
3. Split the mixture into 6 portions and fill the greased donut pan.
4. Sprinkle bagel seasoning on top.
5. Bake at 375F for 15 to 20 minutes.
6. Remove and serve.

Nutritional Facts Per Serving

- Calories: 218
- Fat: 16g
- Carb: 5g
- Protein: 14g

Onion Bagels

Prep time: 15 minutes
Cook time: 30 minutes
Servings: 6

Ingredients

- 2 tbsp. coconut flour
- 3 tbsp. flaxseed meal
- ½ tsp. baking powder
- 4 eggs, separated
- 1 tsp. dried minced onion

Method

1. Preheat the oven to 325F. Grease a donut pan with cooking spray.
2. Sift the flax meal, coconut flour, minced onion, and baking powder.
3. Whip the egg whites until foamy. Slowly whisk in the yolks and dry mixture. Let the dough thicken for 5 to 10 minutes.
4. Scoop into the molds and sprinkle with a portion of dried onion to your liking.
5. Bake for 30 minutes, or until golden brown.
6. Cool and serve.

Nutritional Facts Per Serving

- Calories: 78
- Fat: 5g
- Carb: 1g
- Protein: 5g

Low-Carb Coconut Bagel

Prep time: 15 minutes
Cook time: 25 minutes
Servings: 12

Ingredients

- 1 cup protein powder, unflavored
- 1/3 cup coconut flour
- 1 tsp. baking powder
- ½ tsp. sea salt
- ¼ cup ground flaxseed
- 1/3 cup sour cream
- 8 eggs

Seasoning topping

- 1 tsp. dried parsley
- 1 tsp. dried oregano
- 1 tsp. dried minced onion
- ½ tsp. garlic powder
- ½ tsp. dried basil
- ½ tsp. sea salt

Method

1. Preheat the oven to 350F.
2. In a mixer, blend sour cream and eggs until well combined.
3. Whisk together the flaxseed, salt, baking powder, protein powder, and coconut flour in a bowl.
4. Gently mix the dry ingredients into the wet ingredients until well blended.
5. Whisk the topping seasoning together in a small bowl. Set aside.
6. Grease 2 donut pans that can contain 6 donuts each.
7. Sprinkle pan with about 1 tsp. topping seasoning and evenly pour batter into each.
8. Sprinkle the top of each bagel evenly with the rest of the seasoning mixture.
9. Bake in the oven for 25 minutes, or until golden brown.
10. Cool and serve.

Nutritional Facts Per Serving

- Calories: 134
- Fat: 6.8g
- Carb: 4.2g
- Protein: 12.1g

Garlic Breakfast Bagels

Prep time: 10 minutes
Cook time: 15 minutes
Servings: 6

Ingredients

- ½ cup coconut flour, sifted
- 6 whole eggs
- 1 ½ tsp. garlic powder
- 1/3 cup butter, melted
- ½ tsp. salt
- ½ tsp. baking powder

Method

1. Preheat the oven to 400F.
2. Grease bagel pan and set aside.
3. In a bowl, whisk in eggs, garlic powder, butter, and salt.
4. Add coconut flour and baking powder to the egg mix. Whisk to make a batter.
5. Pour batter into bagel pan.
6. Bake for 15 minutes.
7. Remove from the oven and cool.
8. Serve.

Nutritional Facts Per Serving

- Calories: 193
- Fat: 15g
- Carb: 4.6g
- Protein: 7.7g

Donuts

Prep time: 10 minutes
Cook time: 15 minutes
Servings: 24

Ingredients

- ¼ cup Erythritol
- ¼ cup flaxseed meal
- ¾ cup almond flour
- 1 tsp. baking powder
- 1 tsp. vanilla extract
- 2 eggs
- 3 tbsp. coconut oil
- ¼ cup coconut milk
- 20 drops of red food coloring
- A pinch of salt
- 1 tbsp. cocoa powder

Method

1. In a bowl, mix almond flour, flaxseed meal, cocoa powder, baking powder, salt, and erythritol. Mix.
2. In another bowl, mix coconut oil with coconut milk, vanilla extract, food coloring, eggs, and stir.
3. Combine 2 mixtures and stir using a hand mixer.
4. Transfer to a piping bag and shape 12 donuts on a baking sheet.
5. Place in an oven at 350F. Bake for 15 minutes.
6. Serve.

Nutritional Facts Per Serving

- Calories: 41
- Fat: 3.7g
- Carb: 3g
- Protein: 1g

CHAPTER 7 DIABETIC BUNS

Sweet Buns

Prep time: 10 minutes
Cook time: 30 minutes
Servings: 8

Ingredients

- ½ cup coconut flour
- 1/3 cup psyllium husks
- 2 tbsp. Swerve
- 1 tsp. baking powder
- A pinch of salt
- ½ tsp. cinnamon
- ½ tsp. cloves, ground
- 4 eggs
- 2 tbsp. chocolate chips, unsweetened
- 1 cup hot water

Method

1. In a bowl, mix flour, Swerve, psyllium husks, baking powder, salt, cinnamon, cloves, and chocolate chips, and stir well.
2. Add water and egg, stir well until you obtain a dough, shape 8 buns and arrange them on a lined baking sheet.
3. Bake in the oven at 350F for 25-30 minutes.
4. Serve.

Nutritional Facts Per Serving

- Calories: 100
- Fat: 3g
- Carb: 6g
- Protein: 6g

Swedish Buns

Prep time: 15 minutes
Cook time: 25 minutes
Servings: 4

Ingredients

- ¾ cup almond flour
- 1 tbsp. whole flax seeds
- 2 tbsp. psyllium husk powder
- 1 tbsp. shelled sunflower seeds
- ½ tsp. salt
- 1 tsp. baking powder
- 2 eggs
- 2 tbsp. avocado oil
- ½ cup sour cream

Method

1. Preheat the oven to 400F.
2. In a bowl, add almond flour, seeds, psyllium husk powder, salt, and baking powder. Mix well.
3. Add eggs, avocado oil, and sour cream into the mixture and mix until fully combined.
4. Let dough sit for 5 minutes then cut into 4 portions.
5. Shape each dough portion into a ball and transfer onto a parchment paper lined 9" round cake pan.
6. Place cake pan into the preheated oven. Bake for 20 to 25 minutes or until browned.
7. Cool, slice, and serve.

Nutritional Facts Per Serving

- Calories: 257
- Fat: 21g
- Carb: 8g
- Protein: 10g

Sandwich Rolls

Prep time: 10 minutes
Cook time: 14 minutes
Servings: 6

Ingredients

- 1 cup almond flour
- ¼ tsp. baking soda
- ½ tsp. salt
- 4 tbsp. unsalted butter, melted
- 4 eggs
- 2 tbsp. almond milk
- 2 tbsp. topping (poppy seeds or sesame seeds)

Method

1. Preheat the oven to 425F.
2. Combine the almond flour, baking soda, and salt in a bowl and blend well.
3. Add the wet ingredients to the bowl and mix well.
4. Divide the batter among a muffin top baking pan. Sprinkle with topping.
5. Bake for 12 to 14 minutes.
6. Cool and serve.

Nutritional Facts Per Serving

- Calories: 143
- Fat: 13g
- Carb: 1g
- Protein: 5g

Almond Buns

Prep time: 5 minutes
Cook time: 26 minutes
Servings: 6

Ingredients

- 1 tsp. onion flakes
- 1 tbsp. black sesame seeds
- 1 tbsp. white sesame seeds
- 1 tsp. rosemary
- 3.5 oz. almond flour
- ½ tsp. Himalayan salt
- 4 eggs
- 4 tbsp. unsalted butter

Method

1. Preheat the oven to 430F.
2. Add the eggs and melted butter inside a stick blender beaker.
3. Add the remaining ingredients and place the stick blender into the beaker. Pulse until batter is fully mixed.
4. Take 6 silicone jumbo muffin molds and evenly pour the batter. If desired, sprinkle top of each bun with extra sesame seeds.
5. Bake in the oven at 430F for 26 minutes.
6. Cool, slice, and serve.

Nutritional Facts Per Serving

- Calories: 230
- Fat: 20.82g
- Carb: 3.99g
- Protein: 8.45g

Almond Flour Apple Bread Rolls

Prep time: 10 minutes
Cook time: 30 minutes
Servings: 6

Ingredients

- 1 cup boiling water or as needed
- 2 cups almond flour
- ½ cup ground flaxseed
- 4 tbsp. psyllium husk powder
- 1 tbsp. baking powder
- 2 tbsp. olive oil
- 2 eggs
- 1 tbsp. apple cider vinegar
- ½ tsp. salt

Method

1. Preheat the oven to 350F.
2. In a bowl, mix together the almond flour, baking powder, psyllium husk powder, flax-seed flour, and salt.
3. Add the olive oil and eggs and blend until mixture resembles breadcrumbs, then mix in the apple cider vinegar.
4. Slowly add boiling water and mix into the mixture. Let stand for half an hour to firm up.
5. Line parchment paper over the baking tray.
6. Using your hands, make a ball of the dough.
7. Transfer dough balls on a baking tray and bake for 30 minutes, or until firm and golden.

Nutritional Facts Per Serving

- Calories: 301
- Fat: 24.1g
- Carb: 5g
- Protein: 11g

Buttery Rolls

Prep time: 5 minutes
Cook time: 25 minutes
Servings: 10

Ingredients

- ¼ tsp. pink Himalayan salt
- ½ cup coconut flour
- ½ tsp. baking powder
- ¾ cup water
- 2 tbsp. psyllium husk powder
- 4 eggs
- 4 tbsp. butter

Method

1. In a bowl, combine the coconut flour, psyllium husk powder, salt, and baking powder.
2. Add the eggs into another bowl and beat together, then add in the water, melted butter, and mix well.
3. Combine the psyllium husk powder mixture with egg mixture. Mix until you get a dough.
4. Mold the dough into 10 rolls then arrange on a parchment-lined baking sheet then place into a 350F preheated oven.
5. Bake for 30 to 35 minutes.
6. Cool and serve.

Nutritional Facts Per Serving

- Calories: 102
- Fat: 7g
- Carb: 5.8g
- Protein: 3g

Cheesy Rolls

Prep time: 5 minutes
Cook time: 10 minutes
Servings: 6

Ingredients

- ¼ cup almond flour
- 1 ounce cream cheese
- 1 cup shredded mozzarella
- ¼ cup ground flaxseed
- ½ tsp. baking soda
- 1 egg
- Sesame seeds

Method

1. Preheat the oven to 400F.
2. Line a baking sheet with parchment paper. Set aside.
3. In a bowl, add cream cheese and mozzarella and microwave for 1 minute or until melted.
4. Stir cheese mixture until a smooth consistency is achieved.
5. Add egg into the cheese mixture and stir to combine.
6. Add almond flour, ground flaxseed, and baking soda into another bowl and combine.
7. Add the egg and cheese mixture into the flour mixture and stir until a sticky dough is formed.
8. Mold the dough into six balls.
9. Sprinkle sesame seeds over each dough ball. Place on the prepared baking sheet.
10. Transfer dough ball into the preheated oven and baking for 10 to 12 minutes, or until golden.
11. Cool and serve.

Nutritional Facts Per Serving

- Calories: 219
- Fat: 18g
- Carb: 2.3g
- Protein: 10.7g

Buns with Cottage Cheese

Prep time: 10 minutes
Cook time: 15 minutes
Servings: 8

Ingredients

- 2 eggs
- 3 oz. almond flour
- 1 oz. Erythritol
- 1/8 tsp. Stevia
- Cinnamon and vanilla extract to taste

Filling

- 5 ½ oz. cottage cheese
- 1 egg
- Cinnamon and vanilla extract to taste

Method

1. Prepare the filling by mixing its ingredients in a bowl.
2. Combine eggs with almond flour, blend until smooth. Add erythritol, stevia, and flavors to taste.
3. Spoon 1 Tbsp. dough into silicone cups. Spoon about 1 tsp. filling on top, and bake at 365F for 15 minutes.

Nutritional Facts Per Serving

- Calories: 77
- Fat: 5.2g
- Carb: 6.7g
- Protein: 5.8g

Egg and Seed Buns

Prep time: 10 minutes
Cook time: 50 minutes
Servings: 8

Ingredients

- 2 egg whites
- 1 cup sunflower seeds, ground
- ¼ cup flax seeds, ground
- 5 tbsp. psyllium husks
- 1 cup boiling hot water
- 2 tsp. baking powder
- Salt to taste

Method

1. Combine all the dry ingredients.
2. Add the egg whites and blend until smooth.
3. Add boiling water and keep whisking.
4. Line a baking sheet with parchment paper. Drop the dough on it one spoonful at a time to form buns.
5. Bake at 356F for 50 minutes.
6. Serve.

Nutritional Facts Per Serving

- Calories: 91
- Fat: 4.2g
- Carb: 12.1g
- Protein: 3.3g

CHAPTER 8 DIABETIC FRIENDLY CRACKERS

Sesame Almond Crackers

Prep time: 10 minutes
Cook time: 24 minutes
Servings: 8

Ingredients

- 8 tbsp. unsalted butter, softened slightly
- 2 egg whites
- ½ tsp. salt
- ¼ tsp. black pepper
- 2 ¼ cups almond flour
- 2 tbsp. sesame seeds

Method

1. Preheat the oven to 350F.
2. In a bowl, beat together the egg whites, butter, salt, and black pepper.
3. Stir in the almond flour and sesame seeds.
4. Roll the dough out between two pieces of parchment paper to a rectangle.
5. Peel off the top parchment paper and place the dough on a sheet pan.
6. Cut the dough into crackers with a pizza cutter.
7. Bake for 18 to 24 minutes, or until golden, rotating the tray halfway through.
8. Serve.

Nutritional Facts Per Serving

- Calories: 299
- Fat: 28g
- Carb: 4g
- Protein: 8g

Goat Cheese Crackers

Prep time: 5 minutes
Cook time: 20 minutes
Servings: 12

Ingredients

- 6 oz. goat cheese
- ½ cup coconut flour
- 4 tbsp. butter
- 2 tbsp. fresh rosemary
- 1 tsp. baking powder

Method

1. In a food processor, combine all ingredients. Mix until smooth.
2. Roll out the dough with a rolling pin to about ¼ to ½ inch thick and cut out the crackers with a knife or cookie cutter.
3. Line a baking sheet with parchment paper. Place the crackers on it.
4. Bake at 380F for 15 to 20 minutes.

Nutritional Facts Per Serving

- Calories: 99
- Fat: 8g
- Carb: 2g
- Protein: 4g

Savory Italian Crackers

Prep time: 10 minutes
Cook time: 15 minutes
Servings: 30

Ingredients

- 1 ½ cup almond flour
- ¼ tsp. garlic powder
- ½ tsp. onion powder
- ½ tsp. thyme
- ¼ tsp. basil
- ¼ tsp. oregano
- ¾ tsp. salt
- 1 egg
- 2 tbsp. olive oil

Method

1. Preheat the oven to 350F. Line a baking sheet with parchment paper. Set aside.
2. Combine all the ingredients in a food processor until dough forms.
3. Form the dough into a log. Slice into thin crackers. Arrange the crackers onto the prepared baking sheet. Bake for 10 to 15 minutes.
4. Cool and serve.

Nutritional Facts Per Serving

- Calories: 63.5
- Fat: 5.8g
- Carb: 1.8g
- Protein: 2.1g

Cheese Spinach Crackers

Prep time: 15 minutes
Cook time: 25 minutes
Servings: 16

Ingredients

- 1 ½ cups almond flour
- 5 cups fresh spinach
- ½ cup flax meal
- ¼ cup coconut flour
- ½ tsp. ground cumin
- ¼ cup butter
- ½ cup parmesan cheese, grated
- ½ tsp. flaked chili peppers, dried
- ½ tsp. salt

Method

1. Bring water to boil in a saucepan.
2. Add spinach and cook for 1 minute.
3. Add cooked spinach leaves into a cold water bowl to stop the cooking process.
4. Squeeze out the water from the spinach leaves and drain.
5. Process the spinach in a food processor and process until a smooth consistency is reached.
6. In the meantime, add almond flour, coconut flour, flax meal, cumin, chili flakes, salt, and parmesan cheese into the bowl and mix well.
7. Add softened butter and spinach into the flour mixture and mix to combine well.
8. Transfer dough into a refrigerator. Wrap in foil and keep for 1 hour.
9. Preheat oven to 400F.
10. Remove the foil wrapping and transfer the dough to a parchment paper lined baking sheet.
11. Top dough with second parchment paper piece and roll dough with a rolling pin until the dough is ¼ inch thick.
12. Slice dough into 16 even pieces, using a pizza cutter.
13. Transfer baking sheet into the preheated oven and bake dough for 18 to 20 minutes.
14. For a crunchier texture, adjust oven temperature to 260F and bake for 15 to 20 minutes more.

Nutritional Facts Per Serving

- Calories: 126
- Fat: 10.9g
- Carb: 1.4g
- Protein: 4.5g

Flavors Mascarpone Tart

Prep time: 15 minutes
Cook time: 15 minutes
Servings: 8

Ingredients for the crust

- 1 egg
- 1 tsp. vanilla
- ¼ cup Swerve
- ¼ cup butter, melted
- 2 cups almond flour

For the filling

- 2 tbsp. heavy cream
- ¼ cup Swerve
- 6 oz. mascarpone cheese
- ¾ cup lemon curd

Method

1. Spray the tart pan with cooking spray. Set aside.
2. Preheat the oven to 350F.
3. Add almond flour, vanilla, Swerve, egg, and butter into the food processor and process until it forms a dough.
4. Add the dough into the prepared tart pan and spread out evenly.
5. Prick the crust with a fork and cover with parchment paper and dried beans.
6. Bake in the oven for 15 minutes.
7. Remove from the oven. Set aside to cool completely.
8. Add lemon curd, heavy cream, Swerve, and mascarpone into the food processor and process until smooth and creamy.
9. Pour filling mixture into the baked crust and spread evenly. Place in the refrigerator for 2 hours.
10. Cut into slices and serve.

Nutritional Facts Per Serving

- Calories: 369
- Fat: 24g
- Carb: 6g
- Protein: 9g

CHAPTER 10 OTHER DIABETIC BAKERY RECIPES

Blueberry Scones

Prep time: 10 minutes
Cook time: 10 minutes
Servings: 10

Ingredients

- ½ cup coconut flour
- 1 cup blueberries
- 2 eggs
- ½ cup heavy cream
- ½ cup butter
- ½ cup almond flour
- A pinch of salt
- 5 tbsp. Stevia
- 2 tsp. vanilla extract
- 2 tsp. baking powder

Method

1. In a bowl, mix coconut flour and almond flour, salt, baking powder, blueberries, and stir well.
2. In another bowl, mix butter, heavy cream, vanilla extract, stevia, eggs, and stir well.
3. Combine the 2 mixtures and stir until you get a dough.
4. Shape 10 triangles from mixture and place on a lined baking sheet.
5. Place in an oven at 350F. Bake for 10 minutes.
6. Serve.

Nutritional Facts Per Serving

- Calories: 199
- Fat: 16g
- Carb: 10.6g
- Protein: 4g

Parmesan-Thyme Popovers

Prep time: 10 minutes
Cook time: 15 minutes
Servings: 6

Ingredients

- 4 eggs
- ½ cup coconut milk
- 2 tbsp. coconut flour
- Pinch salt
- 1 tbsp. parmesan cheese
- 1 tbsp. chopped fresh thyme

Method

1. Preheat the oven to 425F.
2. Add all the ingredients to a bowl and whisk until fully blended.
3. Fill nonstick popover sleeves 2/3 with butter.
4. Bake for 15 minutes. Or until popovers begin to brown on top.
5. Cool and serve.

Nutritional Facts Per Serving

- Calories: 64
- Fat: 34g
- Carb: 2g
- Protein: 3g

Savory Waffles

Prep time: 10 minutes
Cook time: 20 minutes
Servings: 4

Ingredients

- 4 eggs
- 1 tsp. olive oil
- ½ cup sliced scallions
- ¾ cup grated pepper Jack cheese
- ¼ tsp. baking soda
- Pinch salt
- 2 tbsp. coconut flour

Method

1. Preheat the waffle iron to medium heat.
2. Mix all the ingredients in a bowl. Let the batter sit for a few minutes and mix once more.
3. Scoop ½ cup to 1-cup batter (depending on the size of the waffle iron) and pour onto the iron. Cook according to the manufacturer's directions.
4. Serve warm.

Nutritional Facts Per Serving

- Calories: 183
- Fat: 13g
- Carb: 4g
- Protein: 12g

Breakfast Pizza

Prep time: 10 minutes
Cook time: 15 minutes
Servings: 2

Ingredients

- ½ tsp. salt
- 1 tbsp. psyllium husk powder
- 2 cups cauliflower florets, riced
- 2 tbsp. coconut flour
- 3 eggs

Method

1. Preheat the oven to 350F. Line a baking tray with parchment paper.
2. In a bowl, add everything and mix well. Set aside for 5 minutes.
3. Then transfer into the baking tray. Flatten to give pizza dough shape.
4. Bake until golden brown, about 15 minutes.
5. Remove. Top with toppings of your choice.
6. Serve.

Nutritional Facts Per Serving

- Calories: 454
- Fat: 31g
- Carb: 8g
- Protein: 22g

Diabetic Pizza

Prep time: 10 minutes
Cook time: 20 minutes
Servings: 1

Ingredients

- 2 eggs
- 2 tbsp. parmesan cheese
- 1 tbsp. psyllium husk powder
- ½ tsp. Italian seasoning
- Salt to taste
- 2 tsp. frying oil
- 1 ½ ounce mozzarella cheese
- 3 tbsp. tomato sauce
- 1 tbsp. chopped basil

Method

1. In a blender, place the parmesan, psyllium husk powder, Italian seasoning, salt, and two eggs and blend.
2. Heat a large frying pan. Add the oil.
3. Add the mixture to the pan in a large circular shape.
4. Flip once the underside is browning and then remove from the pan.
5. Spoon the tomato sauce onto the pizza crust and spread.
6. Add the cheese and spread over the top of the pizza.
7. Place the pizza into the oven – it is done once the cheese is melted.
8. Top the pizza with basil.

Nutritional Facts Per Serving

- Calories: 459
- Fat: 35g
- Carb: 3.5g
- Protein: 27g

Pepperoni Pizza

Prep time: 5 minutes
Cook time: 10 minutes
Servings: 4

Ingredients

- 8 ounces mozzarella cheese, shredded
- Garlic seasoning to taste
- Italian herb seasoning to taste
- 2 ounces pepperoni, chopped

Method

1. Heat a non-stick skillet over medium heat.
2. When hot, sprinkle in the cheese in an even layer to cover the base of the skillet.
3. Sprinkle over the garlic and herb seasonings as soon as the cheese starts to bubble as well as the pepperoni.
4. When the edges of the pizza begin to brown, and it begins to loosen from the bottom of the skillet, slide the pizza out onto a serving plate.
5. Cool until firm.
6. Slice and serve.

Nutritional Facts Per Serving

- Calories: 241
- Fat: 17.6g
- Carb: 2.2g
- Protein: 17.9g

Cheddar Sausage Biscuits

Prep time: 15 minutes
Cook time: 25 minutes
Servings: 8

Ingredients

- 6 oz. cooked sausage, grease drained, thinly sliced
- ¼ cup water
- ¼ cup heavy cream
- 1 cup shredded sharp white cheddar cheese
- 1 ½ cups almond flour
- ½ tsp. Italian seasoning
- ½ tsp. sea salt
- 1 tbsp. chopped fresh chives
- 2 minced large garlic cloves
- 1 large egg
- 4 oz. softened cream cheese

Method

1. Preheat the oven to 350F.
2. Using a hand mixer on low speed, whip the eggs and cream cheese in a bowl.
3. Add the garlic, chives, sea salt, Italian seasoning, then mix into the egg cheese mixture.
4. Add the water, almond flour, heavy cream, and cheddar cheese. Mix well.
5. Slowly mix in the sausage into the mixture using a spatula.
6. Lightly grease muffin pan.
7. Drop a heap mold of dough into 8 wells on the muffin top pan.
8. Bake in the oven for 25 minutes.
9. Cool and serve.

Nutritional Facts Per Serving

- Calories: 321
- Fat: 28g
- Carb: 3.5g
- Protein: 13g

Pizza with a Chicken Crust

Prep time: 10 minutes
Cook time: 20 minutes
Servings: 8

Ingredients

- 7 ounces chicken breast meat, ground
- 7 ounces mozzarella cheese, grated
- 1 tsp. garlic salt
- 1 tsp. dried basil
- 4 tbsp. pizza topping sauce, no sugar added
- 4 ounces cheddar cheese, grated
- 12 slices pepperoni
- Fresh basil leaves

Method

1. Pre-heat the oven to 450F.
2. Line a 12-inch pizza pan with parchment.
3. Mix the chicken, cheese, garlic salt, and dried basil together.
4. Spread into the pizza pan in an even layer and bake in the preheated oven for 10 to 12 minutes.
5. Remove from the oven and cool a little before adding the topping of sauce, cheddar cheese, and pepperoni.
6. Once the topping is on, replace it in the hot oven and cook for 5 to 7 minutes or until hot and bubbly.
7. Remove from the oven. Top with torn basil leaves.
8. Cut and serve.

Nutritional Facts Per Serving

- Calories: 228
- Fat: 14.6g
- Carb: 3g
- Protein: 20.2g

Coconut & Psyllium Pizza Crust

Prep time: 10 minutes
Cook time: 25 minutes
Servings: 4

Ingredients

- ¾ cup coconut flour
- ½ tsp. salt
- ½ tsp. baking soda
- 1 cup boiling water
- 1 tsp. powdered garlic
- 1 tsp. apple cider vinegar
- 3 eggs
- 3 tbsp. psyllium husk powder

Method

1. Preheat the oven to 350F.
2. Combine the psyllium husk powder, coconut flour, salt, and powdered garlic in a bowl.
3. Add the baking soda, apple cider vinegar, and eggs into the mixing bowl and combine then pour in the boiling water and mix.
4. Spread out the dough on a parchment paper-lined baking sheet.
5. Bake for 15 to 20 minutes. Or until the edges start turning brown.
6. Top with cheese, sauce, and any other toppings of your choice and return into the oven until the cheese melts.
7. Serve warm.

Nutritional Facts Per Serving

- Calories: 189
- Fat: 7g
- Carb: 6g
- Protein: 8g

Easy Almond Flour Pizza Crust

Prep time: 5 minutes
Cook time: 15 minutes
Servings: 8

Ingredients

- 2 cups almond flour
- 2 eggs
- 2 tbsp. coconut oil, melted
- ½ tsp. sea salt

Method

1. Preheat the oven to 350F. Line a baking sheet with parchment paper.
2. In a bowl, mix the ingredients to make a dough.
3. Form the dough into a ball. Put in between two parchment paper sheets, and roll out the dough to ¼ inch thick.
4. Remove the parchment paper piece on top. Place the crust on a pizza pan. Poke the crust with a toothpick a few times to prevent bubbling.
5. Bake for 15 to 20 minutes or until golden.
6. Top with your preferred toppings.
7. Return to the oven. Bake for 10 to 15 minutes.
8. Serve.

Nutritional Facts Per Serving

- Calories: 211
- Fat: 19g
- Carb: 3g
- Protein: 8g

Pumpkin Pie Coconut Crisps

Prep time: 5 minutes
Cook time: 5 minutes
Servings: 4

Ingredients

- 2 tbsp. coconut oil
- ½ tsp. vanilla extract
- ½ tsp. pumpkin pie spice
- 1 tbsp. granulated Erythritol
- 2 cups unsweetened coconut flakes
- 1/8 tsp. salt

Method

1. Preheat the oven to 350F.
2. Melt the coconut oil in the microwave.
3. Add pumpkin pie spice, vanilla extract, and granulated erythritol to coconut oil and mix well.
4. In a bowl, place the coconut flakes.
5. Pour coconut oil mixture over them and toss to coat.
6. Spread out on a single layer on a cookie sheet and sprinkle with salt.
7. Bake until crispy, about 5 minutes.

Nutritional Facts Per Serving

- Calories: 327
- Fat: 30.4g
- Carb: 4.6g
- Protein: 2.7g

Chocolate Chip Scones

Prep time: 10 minutes
Cook time: 10 minutes
Servings: 8

Ingredients

- 2 cups almond flour
- 1 tsp. baking soda
- ¼ tsp. sea salt
- 1 egg
- 2 tbsp. low-carb sweetener
- 2 tbsp. milk, cream or yogurt
- ½ cup sugar-free chocolate chips

Method

1. Preheat the oven to 350F.
2. In a bowl, add almond flour, baking soda, and salt and blend.
3. Then add the egg, sweetener, milk, and chocolate chips. Blend well.
4. Pat the dough into a ball. Place it on parchment paper.
5. Roll the dough with a rolling pin into a large circle. Slice it into 8 triangular pieces.
6. Place the scones and parchment paper on a baking sheet and separate the scones about 1 inch or so apart.
7. Bake for 7 to 10 minutes. Or until lightly browned.
8. Cool and serve.

Nutritional Facts Per Serving

- Calories: 213
- Fat: 18g
- Carb: 10g
- Protein: 8g

CONCLUSION

This book gives you a detailed introduction into what exactly the Diabetic diet is and what it really means to be in a low-carb and high-fat diet. It also helps you learn that a high-fat diet is actually nutritious to your health. This means that there are healthy fats available that actually work with the diet to get you to your desired weight goal.

Diabetic bread can also be delicious, mouth-watering, simple to plan, and the best part is that it is super healthy for your body.

Printed in Great Britain
by Amazon